BATHROOM REMODELING
A DO-IT-YOURSELFER'S GUIDE

For Rose, For Everything, Forever

No. 3001
$23.95

BATHROOM REMODELING
A DO-IT-YOURSELFER'S GUIDE

PAUL BIANCHINA

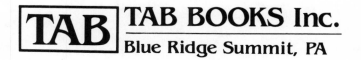

TAB BOOKS Inc.
Blue Ridge Summit, PA

Notices
Jacuzzi is a registered trademark of Jacuzzi Whirlpool Company.
Environment Masterbath and Environment Habitat are trademarks of Kohler Company.
Teflon is a registered trademark of E.I. Du Pont de Nemours & Co.

FIRST EDITION
FIRST PRINTING

Library of Congress Cataloging in Publication Data

Bianchina, Paul
     Bathroom remodeling, a do-it-yourselfer's guide / by Paul
Bianchina

         p.   cm.
     Includes index
         ISBN 0-8306-9001-8   ISBN 0-8306-9301-7 (pbk.)
         1. Bathrooms—Remodeling—Amateurs' manuals. I. Title
     TH3418.B53   1988   88-24775
     643′.52—dc19   CIP

TAB BOOKS Inc. offers software for sale. For information and a catalog, please contact TAB Software Department, Blue Ridge Summit, PA 17294-0850.

Questions regarding the content of this book should be addressed to:

Reader Inquiry Branch
TAB BOOKS Inc.
Blue Ridge Summit, PA 17294-0214

Contents

Acknowledgments

I would like to extend my sincere appreciation to all of the companies and individuals who were so unselfish with their time and materials. Each and every one has made a great contribution to this book. Specifically, and in no particular order, I would like to thank Rose Bianchina for her editing, and especially for her unfailing support and encouragement; Ken and Joy for the pictures of their torn-up bathrooms; Annette Atkins of Kitchen Concepts for her great designs; Mike O'Brien of Western Wood Products Association for his pictures and his vocabulary lessons; Linda E. Kobmann for the great collection of NuTone pictures; Kate Daly of The Pacific Group for all the material on Jacuzzi Whirlpool Baths; Nancy B. Deptolla for her efforts in supplying the beautiful Kohler pictures; Kim Baxley of McKone & Company for all the terrific Wilsonart pictures; Jean Francis of American Olean Tile for all her material; and last but far from least, Kim Tabor—my overworked but cheerfully patient editor at TAB. I would also like to thank:

Amerec, A Division of Nasscor
American Home Lighting Institute
American Olean Tile
American Standard
Andersen Windows
Channellock, Inc.
Congoleum Corporation
Cultured Marble Institute
Diamond Cabinets
E.I. DuPont de Nemours Company, Inc.
Fluidmaster
Glastec
Helo Sauna and Fitness, Inc.
Interbath Inc.
Jacuzzi Whirlpool Bath
Ken and Joy
Kitchen Concepts

Kitchen Kompact, Inc.
Kohler Company
Lattner Boiler Company
Lightolier
Steve Manina, Manina Construction
Medallion Kitchens of Minnesota
Microphor, Inc.
Moen, A Division of Stanadyne
Monarch Mirror Door Company
Nibco, Inc.
Nutone Products
Philips Industries, Inc.
Plumbing Manufacturer's Institute
Ralph Wilson Plastics Company (Wilsonart)
Sancor Industries, Ltd.
Tile Council of America
Tylo Sauna and Steam
Universal-Rundle Corporation
Western Wood Products Association

Introduction

THE BATHROOM—OVER THE YEARS, NO ROOM IN the house has been so important while remaining so stark, utilitarian, and downright unloved. It has been thought of as a room of necessities, not a room of pleasure. With its abundance of plumbing and seemingly oversized fixtures, it has not been a room to spend any more time in than necessary. After all, there really isn't anything you could do to dress up a bathroom, right? Wrong!

The bathroom of today is a far cry from the bathrooms of the past. The purpose is still the same; the plumbing and the fixtures are still there; but many of today's bathrooms are a haven from the outside world. They are a place to relax, to unwind, to soak away tense muscles or exercise off unwanted inches.

More emphasis is being placed on remodeling these days, for the simple fact that people are spending more time at home than ever before. A new or remodeled bathroom is a high priority on almost everyone's list of projects, and with good reason. Many families now have two working adults instead of one, and the stresses and pressures of both career and family life have increased.

As a result, today's bathroom is being viewed as a room with a dual purpose: it must be practical and efficient enough to meet the needs of a fast-paced family life, while still being attractive, inviting, and luxurious enough to afford an oasis of real relaxation at the end of a hectic day. And when you consider that a remodeled bathroom, on average, recovers 75 percent of its initial cost upon resale, and that the addition of a new bathroom recovers up to 110 percent of its cost, the time and effort you lavish on the bathroom makes sound financial sense.

If *efficient*, *attractive*, and *luxurious* do not exactly sound like words that would describe the bathrooms you have in your home, take heart; *Bathroom Remodeling—A Do-It-Yourselfer's Guide* is here to help. You will be taken into beautiful rooms shining with tile and green with plants. You'll learn about basic design principles and see how to guide yourself through the planning and evaluation stages. You'll understand your home's basic plumbing and electrical systems and learn how they work in the bathroom. You'll have a chance to look at different fixtures and faucets, lights and fans, whirlpools and saunas, and much more.

Above all, you will learn how to turn an ordinary, everyday bathroom into a thing of beauty, no matter how small the space or how skimpy the budget. Whether it's a simple facelift with new paint or a room that is completely remodeled from top to bottom, you'll find what you need in the following pages.

From lush plants to skylights, from whirlpool tubs to exercise bikes, today's exciting, exotic, brightly colored bathrooms have finally earned a welcome and respected place in the home. So get out your pencil and paper, shine up your tools, unleash your imagination, and turn the bathroom of your dreams into a reality!

Chapter 1

Bathroom Basics

THE BATHROOM PLAYS A KEY ROLE IN ANY HOME. It sees a tremendous amount of daily activity, yet a great number of bathrooms laid out are poorly and undersized for that much use. Like a kitchen, a bathroom contains large, fixed objects that, once placed, cannot easily be moved. As a result, a poor initial design often will remain that way for the life of the house.

As you work on your ideas and they begin to come together into possible designs, there are a few things you'll want to keep in mind. The enemy of almost all bathroom designs, whether for a new room or a remodeled one, is space. Either the space is poorly planned and inefficiently utilized, or else there's simply not enough space with which to do anything.

Bathrooms are usually small in comparison to the other rooms in the house. Sometimes they are too small to handle much activity efficiently and comfortably. You might have to add additional room to your bathroom to accomplish your remodeling plans. However, having ample space to work with is not always the answer. Many very effective and workable bathroom arrangements are done in fairly limited areas.

One of the real keys to a good bathroom design is the way you utilize the space. Part of that success is in knowing what type of bathroom you want and need. If you're constructing a small guest bathroom that will see a limited amount of use, a small amount of space is usually adequate. If your dreams run toward a luxurious master bathroom, however, skimping on the amount of room you have or can make available can often defeat the design before you even get going.

Much of what you will be wrestling with in your initial designs is fixture location. The bathroom, despite its limited area, is packed with more plumbing than any other room in the house. The plumbing layout and the placement of the fixtures dictate the layout of the remodeled bathroom to a great degree.

Changing fixture locations is time consuming and relatively expensive, especially if you're hiring out the plumbing chores. In homes with wood floors, this work might include cutting and reinforcing joists or even changing the layout of some of the floor framing. If your home has a concrete slab floor, the plumbing was placed in the floor first and the concrete poured around it. As a result, the floor might need to be broken into to gain the necessary access to make any location changes.

By no means should this labor keep you from constructing the type bathroom you really want. Remodeling to achieve a room that falls short of your expectations is little better than not remodeling at all. Just bear these restrictions in mind as you plan, and only consider moving fixture locations (especially the toilet) if the alteration is truly a key feature of the new design.

TYPES OF BATHROOMS

Before you get too far into your own plans, it helps to have a clear understanding of what the different types of bathrooms are. This understanding will help to refine your thinking and planning, and will get you started in the right direction.

There are really no "standard" sizes for bathrooms, and as mentioned earlier, most are undersized for the amount of use they receive. With the following bathroom types are some average sizes that you can use as a guide for your own designs.

Compartmentalized Bathrooms

Designers often employ compartmentalization to get more use out of one room. This type of design uses walls and doors to separate the bathroom's washing facilities from those facilities requiring more privacy, such as the shower and toilet. Because of this feature, more than one person at a time can use the bathroom. (See Fig. 1-1.)

You can use compartmentalization with many different bathroom types, although a space of approximately 6 × 7 feet is considered by most designers to be the very minimum area that can be effectively compartmentalized. Separate bathrooms to meet the needs of family members and guests are usually preferable, but are not always possible. Compartmentalizing the room to serve a dual purpose, or even just to better apportion the available space, might offer the perfect solution to your remodeling needs.

Individual Bathroom

Also called a *single bathroom* (Fig. 1-2), the individual bathroom is the most common type found in residential construction. It contains the three major bathroom fixtures—sink, toilet, and tub (or shower)—and is intended to be occupied and used by only one person at a time. In many homes that

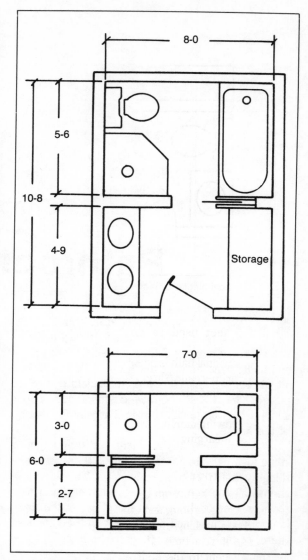

Fig. 1-1. Using a cross wall and pocket door to compartmentalize a family bathroom (top) and a small master bathroom (bottom).

lack a separate guest or half bath, the individual bath also serves the needs of guests.

The individual bath is typically centrally located in the home, and in smaller houses it might be the only bathroom. Typically, the least amount of room you'll find is 5 × 6 feet, or 30 square feet. Some of the more common sizes are 5 × 7 and 5 × 8 feet. The standard bathtub is 5 feet long, so often you

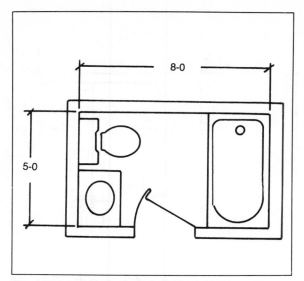

Fig. 1-2. A typical single, or individual, bathroom.

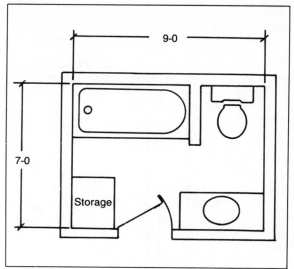

Fig. 1-3. An average-sized family bathroom, with a combination tub/shower, a vanity cabinet, and a separate storage cabinet.

will find 5 feet used as one dimension of the bathroom.

The individual bath is adequate for a small home with two or perhaps three occupants. A larger family would find this one small bathroom inadequate. If you're remodeling or adding on to accommodate a growing family, you'll want to give serious thought to enlarging the room or adding another bathroom.

Family Bathroom

The family bathroom (Fig. 1-3), is larger than the individual bathroom, and often features compartmentalization to allow more than one family member to use it at a time. It is usually conveniently located adjacent to the bedrooms, and serves the needs of most or all of the family. It commonly does double duty by serving the needs of guests.

Typically, the family bathroom contains two sinks in the front part of the room, with a toilet and a bathtub or combination shower/bath in the rear. In homes with a small master or guest bathroom, this room might contain the only bathtub in the house.

In some designs, the family bathroom will be placed between two bedrooms, with a door opening into it from each of the two rooms. An additional

door from a hallway or "living" portion of the home also might be included. The more room you have to work with, the greater the number of design options you'll have.

Master Bathroom

The master bathroom (Fig. 1-4), is intended to serve only the needs of the "master" and "mistress" of the house. It is located off the master bedroom to keep it separate and private from the rest of the family. The master bedroom, bathroom, and dressing areas often combine to create what is called the *master suite*, a very popular feature in larger homes. A home containing a master bathroom also will contain at least one other bathroom for use by the family and guests.

Sizes for the master bathroom vary tremendously. Some rooms might only be 4 × 5 feet or smaller, containing only a small sink, toilet, and stall shower. At the other end of the spectrum, the master bath might be 150 square feet or more. The master bathroom is the least utilitarian of all the bathroom types. It is here that the greatest variety of size, style, and luxury will be found.

What you choose to encompass in the master bathroom is a matter of personal choice. Many mas-

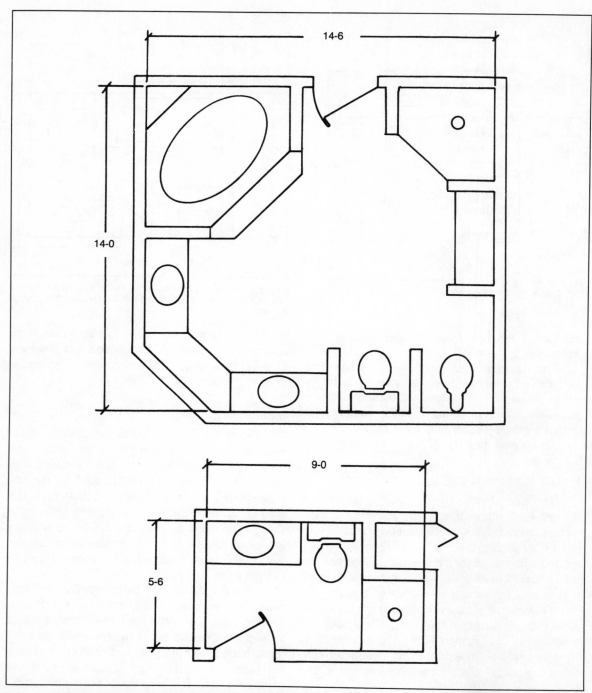

Fig. 1-4. This spacious master bathroom (top) offers a whirlpool bath in a raised platform; a separate stall shower; individual vanities and sinks with a makeup table in between; a toilet and bidet in separate stalls; and ample open storage. The more compact room (bottom) still offers a private area off the master bedroom.

ter bathrooms feature "his and hers" facilities, including two sinks and perhaps two toilets in distinctly separated areas. It might include only a stall shower, offer a combination shower/bath or, in the larger rooms, have both a stall shower and a bathtub. Depending on your tastes and budget, other popular master bathroom options are a bidet, a whirlpool bath, a soaking bath, an oversized bathtub that will accommodate two people, or even a sauna or the addition of steam-generating equipment within the shower stall. Telephones, stereo equipment, and even televisions are not uncommon in today's luxurious master bathroom retreats.

Many larger master bathrooms are being designed to include an exercise area (Fig. 1-5), garden area (Fig. 1-6), or plush, comfortable space for reclining and reading. In keeping with the trend toward separate his and hers facilities in the larger master suites, you also might wish to provide individual dressing areas with separate standard or walk-in closets.

Half Bathroom

The half bathroom (Fig. 1-7), also called a *powder room* or *lavatory*, is so named because it pro-

Fig. 1-5. This bath is part of a large master suite, and offers a whirlpool tub and stall shower, an exercise area, a large storage closet, and access to a private deck through the French door at the left (Courtesy of Universal-Rundle Corporation).

Fig. 1-6. Another lavish master suite, with an enclosed garden area (upper left), a day bed (lower left), and a tremendous amount of elegantly-appointed open space (Courtesy of American Standard).

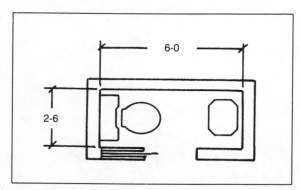

Fig. 1-7. This compact half-bathroom with toilet and pedestal sink is a good example of what can be done in a small area.

vides only a sink and toilet, with no shower or bathtub. It is used to provide the convenience of additional facilities in various parts of the home, particularly on one floor of a two-story house when the family bathroom is on the other floor.

One of the nice things about the half bath is that it can be installed just about anywhere. Most designers use 3 × 4 feet as a standard size, although with careful planning, even smaller spaces have been used with success. Larger spaces, as with any bathroom, will allow you more flexibility with the design, and also will let you incorporate additional storage areas. You can build a half bathroom into any area that can be reached with the necessary plumbing—in the garage or shop, in part of the laundry room, under a set of stairs, in a remodeled basement or attic, or in all or part of an unused closet. If bathroom facilities are limited in your home and the addition of an extra bathtub or shower is not critical, finding a small, convenient area for a half bath might be just what you need.

Three-Quarter Bathroom and Full Bathroom

The three-quarter bathroom is a fairly recent term, and not all designers use it. When you hear a reference to a *three-quarter bath*, the term is being used to indicate a bathroom with a sink, toilet, and stall shower, but no bathtub. (See Fig. 1-8.)

Along with half and three-quarter bathrooms, you will often hear the term *full bathroom*. This term refers to a bathroom with one or more sinks, a toilet, a stall shower, and a bathtub. Bathrooms that have a combination shower/bathtub also are referred to as full bathrooms.

Guest Bathroom

If you have a large home or if you entertain a lot, you might want to create a guest bathroom. By setting aside a bathroom specifically for guests, you keep the room free of the everyday wear and tear of the family, so that it is always fresh and inviting for guests, no matter when they drop in. On the other hand, the guest bathroom does not need to

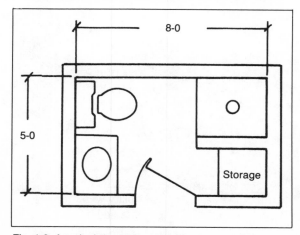

Fig. 1-8. A typical three-quarter bath, with a shower but no bathtub.

be kept only for company; it certainly can be one the family uses also.

The size of the guest bath and its features are matters of personal choice and preference. Typically, a half bath is used for guests, since bathing facilities are not usually necessary. If possible, it should be located near the entry to the home or adjacent to commonly used living areas to avoid the necessity of guests visiting the more private areas of the home.

If you have frequent overnight guests and have a guest bedroom set aside, a small guest bathroom with bathing or showering facilities is a nice touch. It allows your guests privacy, while eliminating additional strain on the family's bathrooms. In this case, the guest bathroom should be close to the guest bedroom, opening directly off it if possible.

SPECIAL-USE BATHROOMS

In several instances, a bathroom is installed to serve the specific needs of one or more members of the family. Specialty bathrooms of this type can by any size, and should be carefully planned and located with those specific needs in mind.

Bathrooms for the Elderly or Disabled

When designing a bathroom to meet the needs of an elderly or disabled member of the family, you must make special plans and carefully consider the layout and fixtures used. You might wish to consult with a designer who is experienced in designs of this type to ensure that the room comfortably and efficiently suits the person's specific needs.

For this type of bathroom you should include an entry door large enough to accommodate a wheelchair. If possible, provide a 2-foot, 10-inch (2-10) or 3-foot (3-0) door for easy maneuvering. Special, extra high toilets can be very helpful, and you should place grab bars wherever necessary, particularly next to the toilet and inside or alongside bathing facilities. (See Fig. 1-9.) You might wish to consider a 3-foot-square or larger stall shower with a built-in or fold-down seat, rather than a bathtub (Fig. 1-10), or install a special waterproof lift mechanism in a standard or oversized tub to facilitate easy entry and exit from the tub.

Fig. 1-9. This full size combination shower/bath is equipped with four sturdy grab bars for safer entrance and exit (Courtesy of Universal-Rundle Corporation).

Fig. 1-10. A well-equipped stall shower for a disabled or elderly person, complete with fold-down seat, hand-held shower, and grab bar (Courtesy of Universal-Rundle Corporation).

WHEELCHAIR LAVATORY 9140.013

VITREOUS CHINA — FOR CONC. ARM SUPPORT.
SHOWN WITH 2238.129 FTG., 3/8 FLEX. SUPPLIES.
7723.018 DRAIN ASSEMBLY, 1-1/4 x 1-1/4 O.D."P" TRAP

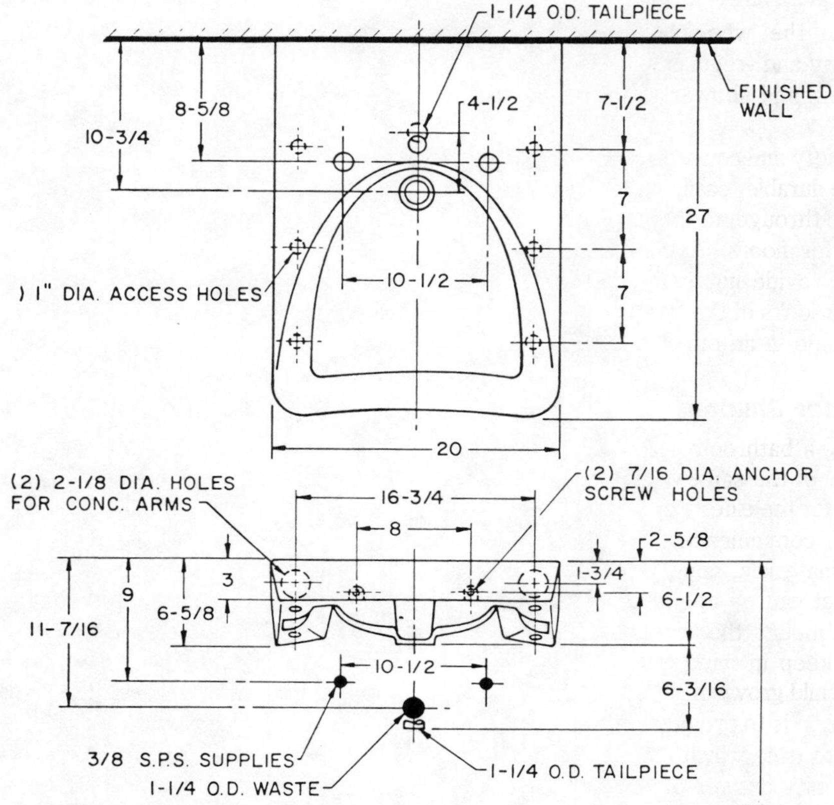

1-1/4 O.D. TAILPIECE

8-5/8

10-3/4

4-1/2

7-1/2

FINISHED WALL

7

27

7

) I" DIA. ACCESS HOLES

10-1/2

20

(2) 2-1/8 DIA. HOLES FOR CONC. ARMS

16-3/4

8

(2) 7/16 DIA. ANCHOR SCREW HOLES

2-5/8

9

3

1-3/4

6-1/2

6-5/8

11-7/16

10-1/2

6-3/16

3/8 S.P.S. SUPPLIES

1-1/4 O.D. WASTE

1-1/4 O.D. TAILPIECE

34 SUGGESTED

NOTE: DIMENSIONS SHOWN FOR LOCATION OF SUPPLIES AND "P" TRAP ARE SUGGESTED.

CONCEALED ARM SUPPORT AS REQUIRED TO BE FURNISHED BY OTHERS.

FINISHED FLOOR

PLUMBER NOTE — Provide suitable reinforcement for all wall supports.

NOTE: FITTINGS NOT INCLUDED WITH FIXTURE AND MUST BE ORDERED SEPARATELY.

IMPORTANT: Dimensions of fixtures are nominal and may vary within the range of tolerances established by ANSI Standards A112.19.2.

These measurements are subject to change or cancellation. No responsibility is assumed for use of superseded of voided leaflets.

AMERICAN STANDARD

L251

71

MAY 1982

Fig. 1-11. An elongated wall-hung sink, specifically designed for use with a wheelchair (Courtesy of American Standard).

10

There are special wall-mounted sinks (Fig. 1-11), that project farther from the wall than ordinary sinks, allowing a wheelchair to be rolled under it with ease. Lever-action or push-button faucets can make the task of using the sink easier. Make sure the undersink plumbing is located so that it does not interfere with the wheelchair's access. Temperature-sensing and -regulating devices are available for the sink and shower to prevent accidental scalding.

Stress safety and convenience in a bathroom of this type. Use durable, easily cleaned materials such as ceramic tile throughout the room, and use a non-slip material for floors. Avoid loose carpeting or throw rugs. Provide higher than normal levels of light, and door locks of the type that can be opened from the outside in an emergency.

Bathrooms for Children

Designing a bathroom specifically for children involves many of the same design techniques used in a bathroom for the elderly or disabled. Once again, stress safety, convenience, and low maintenance with nonslip materials, good levels of lighting, and doorknobs that can be opened from the outside.

You can mount the sink at a lower level if desired, but keep in mind that it will need to be raised as the child grows or if the home is to be sold. A better solution is to provide a large, nonskid step for the child to use, which can be freestanding or built into a vanity drawer or toekick.

Mud Room

A nice feature in many homes is the mud room, which can be included in just about any bathroom design. You should place the mud room adjacent to a garage or on an outside wall, to provide a convenient place for anyone coming in from outside with dirty clothes to change and clean up. The mud room might be just a small area within another bathroom, or it might be a full or half bath with an outside door.

Changing Room

If your home has a swimming pool, spa, or hot tub located outside, a changing room might be a real convenience, saving a lot of wear and tear on the other bathrooms, and eliminating wet feet traipsing through the house. Locate it as near the pool as possible, and include a door from the outside for easy access by the swimmers.

Size and facilities in a changing room vary, but they usually include a toilet, sink, and shower. You can also include a separate changing room with facilities for linen and other storage if desired.

DECIDING WHAT YOU NEED

Bathroom remodeling takes on three basic forms, and each has its inherent advantages and disadvantages. The course your own project takes depends on a variety of factors, including the age and condition of the existing bath, the wants and needs of various family members, and the overall budget you have allotted for completion of the work. Careful planning is essential to ensure the type of bathroom you want and need at a price that is comfortable for you.

Redecorating

The simplest and least expensive form of redoing the bathroom is redecorating. If the bathroom is of adequate size and the fixtures are in relatively good condition, redecorating might be all you need to breathe life into a drab, tired room.

Redecorating might involve little more than a new coat of paint, with a total expenditure of only $20 for materials and a weekend's worth of work. For a few more dollars and a little more effort, you might wish to experiment with other wallcoverings, such as wallpaper or perhaps a combination of both paint and wallpaper.

Redecorating might also involve new floorcovering, which is a fairly minor expense in a room as small as the bathroom. You might wish to strip and paint or stain any cabinets in the room, or perhaps dress them up with new hardware. Additional small storage cabinets can expand the room's usefulness and add a nice decorating touch at the same time.

If you are opting for a new color scheme and the fixtures won't match it, don't immediately think you need to go through the expense of buying new ones, especially if the existing ones are still in good working order. Many companies can completely reglaze bathroom fixtures in a new color, with a result that is virtually indistinguishable from brand new. They can do the work in their shop, or they can visit your home to take care of large items such as the bathtub. Add new faucets, and you've created a beautiful new room for a fraction of the cost of a complete remodeling.

Redesigning

The next step, in terms of time, effort, cost, and results, is to redesign the bathroom, working within the existing space and reusing the existing plumbing locations (See Fig. 1-12.) You can achieve a completely new look in the room while avoiding the two biggest bathroom remodeling expenses: moving the plumbing and adding on space.

Depending on the scope of the project and the size of the budget, redesigning might involve new fixtures, new cabinets, new flooring, ceramic tile walls or counters, new or enlarged windows, a revamped electrical and lighting system, or any combination of these. You might want to leave some of the old components of the room as they are and interwork them with new components, or you might

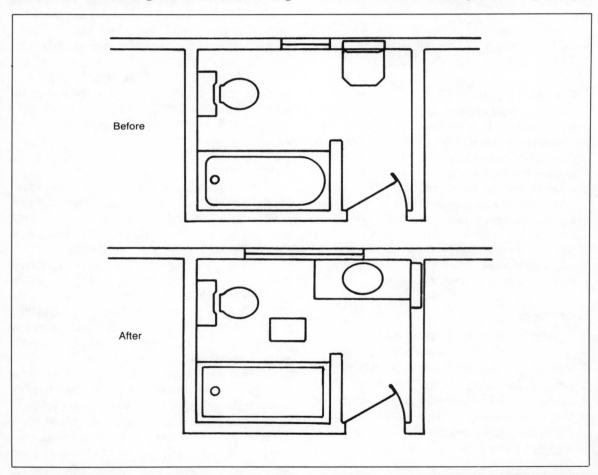

Before

After

Fig. 1-12. Great results often can be achieved in a bathroom without moving the fixture locations. In this room, a new whirlpool tub was installed in place of the old tub; a vanity replaced the existing pedestal sink to gain much needed storage; the old medicine cabinet was removed from behind the sink and a new one was installed to the right of the vanity, allowing the window to be enlarged; and a new toilet and ceiling-mounted fan-heat-light unit completed the makeover.

want to strip the room and begin again as if it were brand new.

The advantages of redesigning are obvious: you can replace outdated or inoperable fixtures, you can add storage space, and you can achieve a new and more efficient room layout, all at moderate cost. The disadvantages are equally apparent: you must work within the existing space, and you have to keep the fixture locations in relatively the same place, although some movement usually is possible.

Remodeling

A true, complete bathroom remodeling is more involved than either redecorating or redesigning. Full remodeling is the most expensive route to take, because it involves the greatest amount of labor and materials. However, it also, offers the greatest amount of design flexibility and allows you to remake the space in any way that you wish. If you cannot achieve a workable floor plan in any other manner, a full remodeling is the only option open to you.

Remodeling a bathroom often will involve moving the fixtures to new locations. This move requires a fairly complete knowledge of plumbing techniques, and might be out of the range of many do-it-yourselfers. Likewise, the complete remodeling project often involves creating additional space in the room, either by adding to the house or by acquiring space from adjacent rooms. Windows and doors often are moved to entirely new locations, fixtures are changed completely, skylights or greenhouses might be added, and the electrical system is reworked completely.

New Bathrooms

There is a fourth general category, to which many of the same rules and ideas you'll find in this book apply. New bathrooms, whether they're for a new house or an addition to an existing home, follow the same guidelines for good design. The advantage to a new bathroom, of course, is that you have a considerably greater degree of design flexibility. While it is still in the planning stages, a new bathroom, in many instances, can be enlarged, altered, or rearranged to any degree necessary to achieve the desired look and floor plan.

If you are in the process of designing a new home or an addition to your present one that will include a bathroom, you still can learn a lot from a close inventory of your existing bathrooms. Size, traffic patterns, fixture arrangement, storage, decor, and other aspects of the existing rooms, good or bad, can offer tremendous guidance for your new design.

Chapter 2

Planning and Design

To BEGIN WORKING ON YOUR NEW BATHROOM, dust off two of the remodeler's most trusted and valuable tools: a pencil and a pad of paper. Long before you'll need a hammer and nails, you'll want to take a close and thorough look at your bathroom project and try to plan for every step. It might seem tedious at first, but it is your best assurance that the work will run smoothly and the final result will be the bathroom you envisioned.

Bathroom design can be tricky. You are trying to pack a lot of things into a small space, and still have that space turn out to be efficient, practical, comfortable, and attractive. It might seem like a tall order at times, and it points out the critical need for careful planning. Any effort you expend at this point will pay itself back many times over in savings of time, frustration, and money. Many bathrooms are only remodeled once or twice in the entire life of the home, so your final design very likely will be one that you are going to be living with for some time to come.

THE JOB FILE

Now is a good time to start a job file. This file might be a shoebox, an empty desk drawer, or a simple file folder—whatever makes you most comfortable.

The idea is to establish one central location for all the paperwork that will build up as you go along.

In your job file, you will want to include all of the lists you'll soon be making; notes and comments from you and your family, no matter how insignificant; pictures and ideas you are clipping from magazines and newspapers; photographs of bathrooms you like; manufacturer's brochures and other literature; bids and estimates from contractors and material suppliers; building permits and code information; receipts and invoices; business cards and telephone numbers; color chips, fabric samples, and wallpaper samples; and anything and everything else pertaining to the job.

ANALYZING THE EXISTING BATHROOM

The easiest and most practical place to begin your planning is by taking a long, hard look at your existing bathroom. Whether you intend to redecorate, remodel within the confines of the existing room, expand the room by adding on or taking space from an adjacent room, or add an entirely new bathroom, the things that you like and dislike about your existing bathroom can provide a lot of very valuable design input.

If your new bathroom will be used by the entire family, then they all should be involved in its design. The likes, dislikes, and general comments of each family member need to be considered seriously if the bathroom design is to be workable and practical for everyone. If the project is a master or guest bathroom, at the very least, heads of the household need to be involved in, the design process but here again, the comments of the entire family will be helpful.

LISTING YOUR LIKES AND DISLIKES

Begin your bathroom analysis by taking a notepad and labeling one sheet of paper "Like" and a second sheet "Dislike." On these two pages, list everything you do and do not like about the bathrooms you now have. List anything and everything that comes to mind, no matter how small or seemingly trivial. Remember that what might seem insignificant to one member of the family might be a real headache for someone else.

Many people will use a room like the bathroom and know that they do not particularly like it, but they might not pay much attention to where those feelings come from. It sometimes takes a critical eye to really take notice of the stained wallpaper, the sticking drawer, or the dripping faucet. With this in mind, you might find it easiest to write your list while in one of the bathrooms. The bathroom might be a little crowded for the entire family, but this process will aid you in making a complete list of the room's faults and virtues.

Your lists should include everything from the size and layout of the room to its decor. Your "Dislike" list might include such items as "too dark," "too small," "peeling paint," "drab decor," "the shower's too small," "not enough towel bars," "no storage space," "cold floors," or even "ugly fixtures."

On the positive side, you might take note of "sunny room," "good amount of counter space," "authentic antique sink and faucet," "nice size mirror," "good lighting for putting on makeup," or a small item like "new shower curtain."

To help you focus your attention on some of the critical areas of the bathroom that you might unconsciously overlook otherwise, refer to the following list as you take your inventory.

Size

How does the room feel to you as you enter and move around in it? Do you need to close the door in order to have access to the vanity? Does the toilet seem too close to the bathtub? Is the size of the shower stall limited by its location?

Layout

Now study the room's general layout. Can you move easily through the room? Is the sink in a convenient spot? Can the towel bars be reached easily from the sink or bathtub? If the vanity has two sinks, can two people comfortably use them at the same time? If it is a family bathroom, is it, or should it be, compartmentalized so one person can have bathing privacy while another uses the sink? Are there enough mirrors? Are they well located? Would a full-length mirror be helpful? Is it important to have a separate makeup mirror?

Layout involves the windows and doors also. Is the door well located? Does it take up valuable floor or wall space when it is open? Is the window in an awkward location? Is the window too small for adequate light or ventilation? Would the installation of a skylight make up the natural light not provided by the window?

Storage

Adequate storage facilities in the bathroom are a necessary and sometimes overlooked aspect of good design. Be certain you analyze both the large and small aspects of the storage situation in your bathrooms. Is there adequate towel storage? Are there enough towel bars, and are they well placed? Is there a medicine cabinet, and is it large enough? If you have a vanity, does it offer enough drawer and cabinet space for everyone who uses the room? Are there holders or storage areas for cosmetics, toothbrushes, water glasses, hair dryers, etc.? Is there a convenient place for face and toilet tissue, both in terms of storage and dispensing?

Your own use of the room might point out some other storage needs and deficiencies. Would you like to be able to store exercise equipment in the room? Are there bulky medical supplies or equipment that need storage? Do you need space to store cleaning supplies, either for the bathroom or perhaps for the entire house?

Fixtures and Faucets

This area of the bathroom, for the most part, is fairly obvious. Are the fixtures in good working order? Are the colors okay, or will they need to be changed to match the new decor? If the colors need to be changed, can the existing fixtures be painted or reglazed, or do they need to be replaced? Would you like to replace two-handle faucets with single-handle ones? Would a sprayer be nice at the sink or in the shower? Would you like a toilet that's quieter or uses less water? Would you like a bidet?

Your analysis of the existing fixtures can go hand in hand with your likes and dislikes about the room's overall layout. For instance, would you like a stall shower and a separate tub in the master bathroom? Is there enough room for it? Would a second sink in the room be helpful? Is there room for it?

Walls, Counters, and Floors

Take a good look at the materials that make up the walls. Are they simply drywall with paint or wallpaper? Would you prefer a covering of ceramic tile, Corian, or synthetic marble? If you would, where would you like these coverings—behind the sink, behind the toilet, next to the tub?

Now turn your attention to the floors. Are they linoleum? Are they ceramic tile? Are they vinyl tile? Are they carpet? Do you like the existing type of covering (ignoring its condition or color), or would you prefer some other type of flooring? Analyze the countertop material the same way and decide if you like the existing type of counter or if you'd prefer something else.

Now is a good time to think about maintenance. Are the existing wall, floor, and countertop materials easy to clean? Would a seamless material like Corian work better for you than ceramic tile? If you have

ceramic tile, would you prefer larger tiles with wider grout lines for easier cleaning? Are there some changes you would like that would make the room more "kid-proof?"

Tub and Shower Enclosures

As you did with the wall coverings, take a critical look at the tub and shower enclosures. Are they fiberglass, or do you wish they were? Would tile or synthetic marble look nicer and be easier to maintain? Does the existing shower consist of out-of-date plastic wall panels? Are you about due for a new shower door, or would you like to get a door to replace the existing shower curtain (or vice versa)?

Electrical Layout

Do not overlook the bathroom's electrical layout, including outlets, light fixtures, and switches. There usually is not that much wiring in a bathroom, but what is there is important to consider, both for safety and convenience. Would you like additional outlets, or like them moved to more convenient locations? Are the existing outlets equipped with ground-fault circuit interrupters (GFCIs)? GFCIs are required by virtually every electrical code, and are important to your family's safety.

Are there adequate levels of light in the room? Are the mirrors well lit, and is there adequate, shadowless light for shaving or applying makeup? Is the shower stall too dark? Are the various light fixtures controlled by separate switches, and are they conveniently located? Are separate light fixtures and switches provided within compartmentalized areas? Do you have fluorescent or incandescent lights, and which would you prefer?

Ventilation and Heat

Two other important and often overlooked areas in the bathroom are ventilation and heat. Adequate ventilation is a must in the bathroom to remove the high levels of moisture present in the air. When you use the bathroom now, do you notice moisture in the air or condensation on the mirrors and windows? Has mold or mildew been a problem? Does your bathroom have a fan? Is it operable and well maintained, and, just as important, does it get used? If you are enlarging the bathroom, will the fan be of adequate size after the remodeling? If children are using the bathroom, is the fan on a timer so that it will shut itself off if they leave the room and forget it?

No one likes a cold bathroom first thing in the morning, so you should consider some form of heat. Is there heat in the bathroom now? Is it safe and adequate for the size of the room? Does your home have central heating, and if so, is the system large enough to bring a new vent into the bathroom? Have you considered a wall heater? Would you like an overhead heater? Will the heater you install be gas or electric? Would a combination fan/heater be the best solution to both problems?

ANALYZING YOUR FAMILY'S NEEDS

The second key element in the evaluation process is analyzing your needs and those of your family. The goal of this analysis is to narrow down and focus your actual wants and needs, so that you can be certain of achieving a bathroom that is as close to ideal for you as possible. It also helps you identify and eliminate budget-draining extras that you do not really need.

The easiest way to start analyzing your needs is by getting out your trusty pencil and paper again. This time, ask yourself some of the following questions, and make note of the answers and comments.

☐ How many people are in your family? Are you expecting any changes (a new baby on the way, a teenager going off to college, etc.)? It's important to identify and plan for upcoming changes.

☐ How many bathroom sinks do you now have? Is that an adequate number to suit your current and anticipated future needs?

☐ How many bathtubs do you have? How many showers do you have? How many toilets do you have? Are these numbers satisfactory for your current and future needs?

☐ Will you need to add a bathroom for a growing family or will enlarging or rearranging the existing bathrooms be sufficient?

☐ What will the additional bathroom need to contain in order to satisfy your family's current and future needs? Where will the added bathroom be located? Does it need to be adjacent to a particular part of the house? Will it be part of a larger addition to the house?

☐ How often do you entertain? Would a half bathroom set aside for guests take the burden off the family's bathrooms, or don't you entertain often enough to justify it?

☐ How often do you have overnight guests? Do you need a three-quarter or full bath for their needs?

☐ Do all or most of the family members need to use the bathrooms at approximately the same time (getting ready for work, getting ready for school, etc.)? Are separate facilities needed to accommodate these needs? Would compartmentalizing one or more of the existing bathrooms ease the strain?

☐ Are there medical needs that one or more of the bathrooms must serve? List exactly what they are, how much space they require, and what utilities are needed to serve special equipment (larger electrical circuits, larger water lines, separate gas lines, etc.).

☐ Do you wish to create an exercise area? List your specific needs, the equipment you will be installing, how much space you'll require, and anything out of the ordinary that should be included in your planning.

☐ Do you need to include closet and/or dressing facilities with the bathrooms? Do these areas require special mirrors or other items?

☐ Do you need to add bathroom storage areas? What items will you be storing?

YOUR "WANTS AND NEEDS" LIST

Now that you have taken a good look at what you like and don't like about your existing bathrooms and you have spent some time identifying your family's needs, it's time to make another list. This list will really help you put things into perspective, and will be a big help to you and your designer. The goal here, as with the other lists, is to identify as closely as possible what you really want and need, while eliminating unnecessary items that would otherwise strain your budget.

This time, divide your paper into three columns and label them "Must Have," "Would Like If Possible," and "Nice, But Can Do Without." This simple list with its three categories will be a surprisingly effective sieve through which to separate your wants and needs. You might wish to get the whole family involved in making up the list, or you might wish to sit down by yourself or with your spouse. However you choose to do it, the trick is to be as honest with yourself as possible in assigning things to the various columns.

In the first column, "Must Have," you'll want to write down everything you've identified that you really must include in the new bathroom. Be as complete and thorough as possible, no matter how small the item. Some of the items on this list might be "an exercise area," "more towel bars," "room for plants," or "a skylight."

In the middle column, "Would Like If Possible," you will want to list those items that you'd like if space and budget permit. This list might include "a bidet," "a bigger window," or "ceramic tile floors." The last column, "Nice, But Can Do Without," might include "a whirlpool bathtub," "a towel warmer," or "gold fixtures."

Be as thorough and honest with yourself as possible, and do not be afraid to assign an item that might seem like an extravagance to the "Must Have" list if it's something you really want. What might be unimportant or an expensive luxury item to one person might be an absolute necessity to you—If it is, by all means list it.

As you can see, listing things in this manner helps your planning immensely, and makes it much easier to determine your budget. You will want to allow enough money for all of the items in the "Must Have" list. You then can take items from the other two lists as your budget allows. You will find probably that few, if any items, from the last column ever make it into the finished bathroom, but at least you'll be assured that it will contain those things you really need.

THE BASICS OF GOOD DESIGN

As you study books and magazines that deal with bathrooms and collect samples of those ideas that appeal to you, you'll begin to notice that there is no real "proper" design for a bathroom. What works for one person in one room might not work for another person or a different room.

Instead, good design is a matter of balancing several elements in a manner that suits your needs and pleases your tastes. The size of the room needs to be considered, as does its shape and the layout of its windows and doors. The number, type, and size of the fixtures you choose is a factor, as is the layout of the existing plumbing and, to a lesser degree, the wiring. Finally, you have the blending of colors and textures in the materials you use, which will come together in a way that's unique to your tastes and lifestyle.

In general, a good design is one that accomplishes the following five things:

☐ The room should be large enough to move around in easily and comfortably. There should be good access to the room, and doors should be positioned so they do not interfere with the fixtures and storage areas.

☐ The fixtures should be laid out for easy access and safe use, with adequate clearance from walls and from each other.

☐ There should be high enough level of artificial light for safe and convenient use. If possible, natural light also should be provided.

☐ The storage space should be sufficient and accessible.

☐ The room should be adequately heated and ventilated.

As mentioned earlier, the two key elements in your design are: the amount of space you have to work with, and the existing layout of the fixtures. The designs that will be the easiest and least expensive to complete are those that retain the original size of the room, the original fixture layout, or both.

If you need to add space, your labor and material costs will rise accordingly. You can gain space either by removing one or more walls to expand the bathroom into adjacent rooms, or if the bathroom is on an exterior wall, by adding onto it. The added space might be a simple garden area or prefabricated

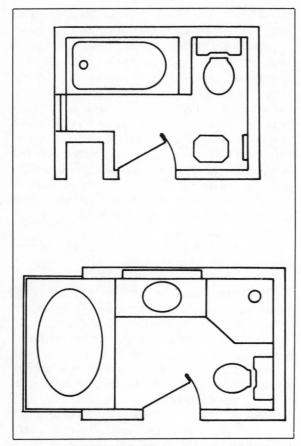

Fig. 2-1. The owners of this bathroom wanted more light and a whirlpool bathtub, but room was limited (top). The necessary space was gained by adding a prefabricated sunspace (bottom left) and expanding the room into the adjacent closet.

sunspace (Fig. 2-1), or it might involve an enlarged or completely new bathroom as part of a larger room addition.

You can usually move a sink two or three feet without too much trouble, depending on the original plumbing layout and local plumbing codes. Likewise, you can add a second sink next to the original one. Tubs and showers require a little more effort to relocate, and moving the toilet often can be a major endeavor. How easy or difficult it will be to move a particular fixture will vary from room to room, depending on how the original plumbing is laid out, if you need for new waste lines and vents, and whether the floor is over a crawl space or a concrete slab.

Here is where your lists really come into play. By clearly defining your needs and the overall goals of your remodeling, you can decide what does and does not need to be done with the room. The trick is to eliminate those aspects of the work that drive the cost up unnecessarily, while still doing whatever work is needed to create the kind of room you really want. Compromises might be necessary along the way, but remember that remodeling to create a design you do not really want is little better than not remodeling at all.

STANDARD BATHROOM LAYOUTS

There are four basic layouts for a bathroom, depending on where the plumbing and fixtures are located. You will find that certain layouts are better suited to a room's size and shape than others:

☐ One-wall: In this layout (Fig. 2-2), all the fixtures are located along one wall of the room. This arrangement works especially well in rooms that are relatively long and narrow. The plumbing is simplified by having it all in the same wall.
☐ Corridor: The fixtures are laid out along two opposite walls. (See Fig. 2-3.) The plumbing is a little more involved, but access is good from one or both ends of the room.

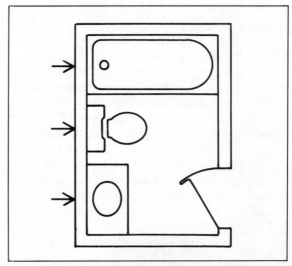

Fig. 2-2. A one-wall bathroom, with the fixtures grouped on the same wall, simplifies plumbing but limits design flexibility.

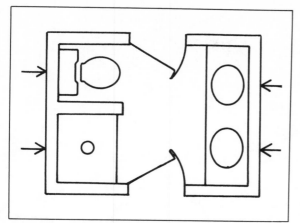

Fig. 2-3. The corridor or two-wall bathroom utilizes fixtures on opposite walls, and is an ideal arrangement when the bathroom must serve two adjacent bedrooms.

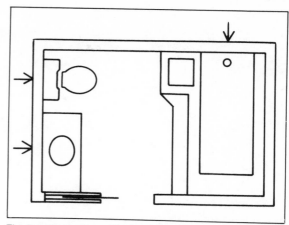

Fig. 2-4. The L-shaped bathroom, with fixtures on two adjacent walls, increases the layout possibilities while remaining relatively easy to plumb.

Fig. 2-5. The U-shaped bathroom offers the greatest amount of design flexibility. Although the plumbing becomes more complicated, this type of layout is a virtual necessity with a bathroom as large as this one.

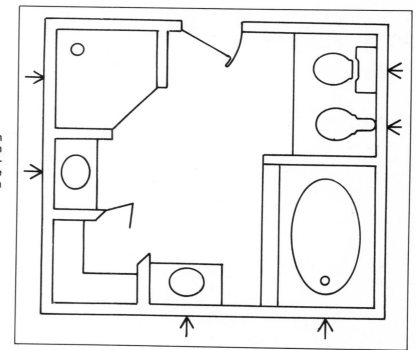

☐ L-Shape: The L-shaped bathroom (Fig. 2-4), has the fixtures arranged on two adjacent walls. This design is common in 5-foot-wide bathrooms. The plumbing is usually all in one wall, but some layouts have plumbing in two walls.

☐ U-Shape: This layout (Fig. 2-5), places the fixtures on three walls. This design especially is suited to square rooms, and usually provides very good access to each fixture. It does, however, require plumbing in three walls.

21

Chapter 3

Laying Out the Bathroom

NOW THAT YOUR DREAMS AND IDEAS ARE BEGIN-ning to take shape and you have narrowed down your list of wants and needs, it is time to start getting some possible layouts drawn on paper. You will see a variety of layouts by making these drawings, and you will be able to play around with fixture locations, wall positions, windows and doors, and storage areas.

DRAWING TO SCALE

In order to have a true perspective of how the room will be laid out and how the various components will relate to each other, you need to use the same guidelines for everything you draw. These common guidelines are known as a *scale*. If you make every item on the drawing the same scale, they all will be in correct proportion to each other.

To make a scale drawing, you will let a certain fraction of an inch equal one foot. For a room as small as a bathroom, a good scale is ½ inch = 1 foot. Therefore, an object that is 1 foot long in actual size would be ½ inch long on the plan. A 2-foot object would be 1 inch long (2 × ½); 3 feet would be 1½ inches, etc. Fractions of a foot are represented the same way: 6 inches actual size (½ foot) would be

¼ inch long on the plan; 3 actual inches would equal ⅛ inch in scale, etc.

You can simplify the preparation of a scale drawing with the use of an *architect's scale*, which is a type of ruler marked in various scale increments. (See Fig. 3-1.) To use a scale of this type, first locate the scale size you wish to draw to—in this case ½ inch = 1 foot, which is referred to simply as ½-inch scale. You will notice a series of numbers evenly spaced to the right of the 0, and a series of smaller numbered marks to the left of 0. The larger spaces to the right are scale feet, and the smaller spaces to the left are scale inches.

To lay off a scale line representing 6 actual feet, simply make a pencil mark at 0, then move to the right to the number 6 and make a second mark. Connect the two marks, and you have a scale line representing 6 actual feet. If the line you wanted to draw was 6 feet 3 inches long, you would mark the 6 to the right of 0, and the 3 to the left of 0. The space between the marks is a scale line 6 feet 3 inches long.

Another, and perhaps simpler, method of drawing to scale is to use graph paper. You can purchase graph paper in a variety of grids, including 2, 4, 8, or 10 squares to the inch. For your purposes, graph

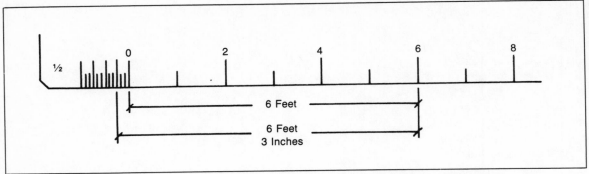

Fig. 3-1. An architect's scale, showing foot and inch measurements in a scale of ½ inch = 1 foot.

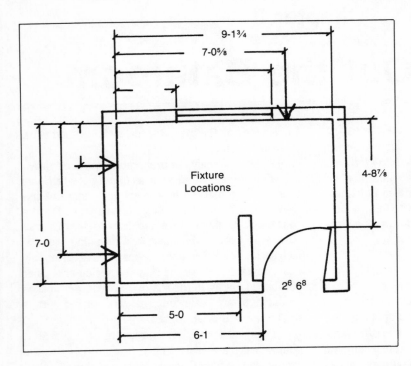

Fixture Locations

Fig. 3-2. Accurate measurements of the existing room and fixture locations is very important during the initial planning stages.

paper with either 4 or 8 squares to the inch will work fine. With 4-square paper, each block on the grid is ¼ inch long, so each would represent 6 inches of actual size when working in ½-inch scale. With 8-square paper, each block is ⅛ inch long, or 3 actual inches in ½-inch scale.

Drawing The Room

The first thing you will want to do is draw the outline of the bathroom itself. (See Fig. 3-2.) If you

are working within the confines of an existing room, carefully measure the inside of the room from wall to wall in both directions, down to the nearest ⅛ inch. Take your measurements along each wall about 6 inches up from the floor, and be certain you measure from wall corner to wall corner, not between the baseboards.

When you have the wall measurements, carefully draw them out in pencil, using either the architect's scale or a sheet of graph paper. Outside the lines, note the actual room measurements for future reference. Next, measure from the door to each adjacent corner and use these measurements to locate the door opening on the drawing. Repeat the procedure for any windows, and draw in their location also. Using a compass, draw in an arc, which represents the swing of the door, from fully closed to fully open.

The final step in drawing an existing bathroom is to show the exact locations of the fixtures, using either an "X" on the plan or an arrow outside the wall boundaries. It is important that you indicate these fixture locations accurately on the drawing so that exact clearances between fixtures can be measured. To verify the locations, measure to the centerline of each fixture from at least two points in the room.

If you are expanding the bathroom into an adjacent space, you'll want to show the existing walls that are going to be removed as dotted lines on your drawing. Then draw in the new walls or the boundaries of the expanded space so that you accurately have the size of the bathroom as it will be after the expansion is complete. Mark the existing fixture locations, also. In the case of an entirely new bath-

room, simply draw in the walls, windows, and doors as they will be after construction.

Drawing the Fixtures

To facilitate a number of possible room layouts, you will find it easiest to make scale drawings of the bathtubs, shower stalls, sinks, vanities, storage areas, exercise equipment, and any other large items that will be placed in the bathroom. Draw each object as though you were looking directly down on it (called a *plan view*), in the same way that the room layout is drawn. The drawings do not need to be fancy, but they do need to be accurately drawn to scale, showing each item's width and length.

Make these drawings using the architect's scale, and draw them on stiff paper or light cardboard. If you are using graph paper instead of the architect's scale, make the drawings on the graph paper and then transfer them to the cardboard. If you wish, you can purchase scale drawing templates of common bathroom fixtures at drafting or art supply stores to simplify the drawing. (See Fig. 3-3.) Be certain the scale of the template you buy is the same as the scale of your drawing. Some stores also

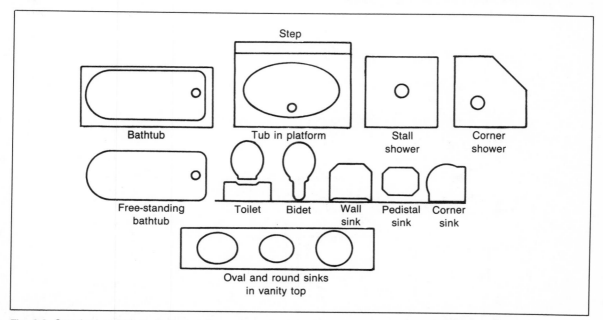

Fig. 3-3. Standard architectural symbols for various plumbing fixtures, drawn with a plumbing template.

carry complete planning kits, with grid paper and predrawn, precut fixtures.

The last step is to carefully cut out each of the drawings. You now have accurate scale fixtures and other components that can be placed on the scale room layout. These scale fixtures allow you to move things around easily and try out different configurations without constantly redrawing the plan.

CLEARANCES

As you begin working with your room plan and fixtures, it is critically important that you be aware of the necessary clearances to maintain, between the fixtures themselves and between each fixture and the walls. Adequate clearance maintains safe and convenient use of the bathroom, and certain minimum clearances are required by the building codes. As you try out different layouts, use your architect's scale to measure clearances, or count the squares on your grid paper.

Following is a list of some commonly accepted bathroom clearances. (See Figs. 3-4 & 3-5.) You'll need to check with your local building officials to verify what clearance codes are in effect in your area. Remember that the codes only specify minimum clearances. Try to provide greater clearance wherever possible to make the bathroom easier to clean and more comfortable to use.

☐ Provide 18 inches between the centerline of the toilet and any wall or fixture next to it.
☐ Provide 30 inches between the front of the toilet and a bathtub or shower, and at least 16 inches between the front of the toilet and the wall opposite it.
☐ Allow the centerline of the sink to be at least 15 inches from an adjacent wall. With double sinks that are side by side, provide at least 30 inches between them, centerline to centerline.
☐ Provide a minimum of 18 inches between the entrance to a stall shower and the opposite wall. Wherever possible, 24 to 30 inches of clearance is much more convenient.
☐ Allow the depth of the vanity countertop to be 20 to 22 inches.

Access for the Disabled

If the bathroom is to be used by someone who is disabled, you need to provide greater room for easy and safe access. (See Fig. 3-6.) Bathroom doors should be 2 feet 8 inches or wider to accommodate a wheelchair. The space between adjacent

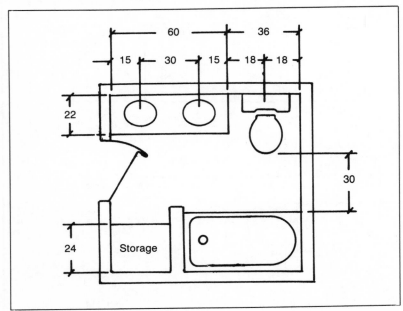

Fig. 3-4. Typical clearances between plumbing fixtures.

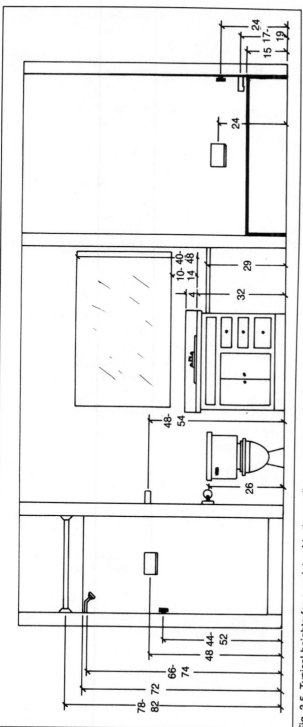

Fig. 3-5. Typical heights for a variety of bathroom fixtures and accessories. These heights can be adjusted to suit the needs and preferences of the people using the room.

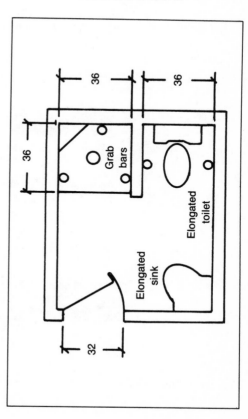

Fig. 3-6. Minimum clearances for a bathroom designed for wheelchair access. The toilet and sink are elongated, a seat is provided in the shower, and grab bars are placed as needed. A ramp, (Figure 4-6A) simplifies entry into the shower (Courtesy of Universal-Rundle Corporation).

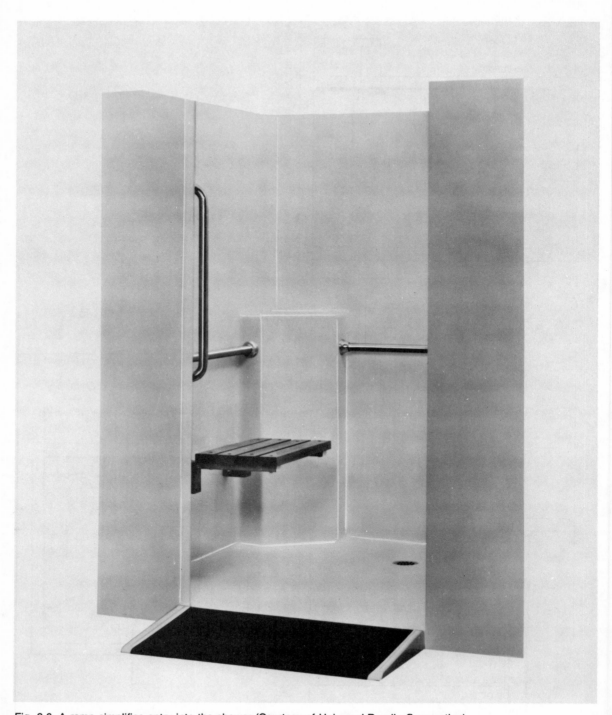

Fig. 3-6. A ramp simplifies entry into the shower (Courtesy of Universal-Rundle Corporation).

walls in front of the toilet should be at least 36 inches wide, with safety grab bars mounted next to it on both sides. Special 18-inch-high toilets should be provided. The rim of the sink should be 34 inches off the floor and the plumbing should be arranged so that it doesn't interfere with a wheelchair's access. Shower stalls should be at least 36 inches square, and grab bars need to be provided for both the shower and the tub.

ROOM LAYOUT GUIDELINES

As mentioned earlier, if you are working with an existing bathroom you will find it easier and less expensive to keep the fixture locations where they are. You might experiment with changing the sink location slightly, doubling the sinks, or compartmentalizing the bathroom to see if these relatively minor changes will satisfy your needs.

If they won't or if you are working with a new bathroom, you will want to begin the new fixture layout by placing the bathtub or shower stall first. These fixtures are the largest in the room and require the most space, so it is easiest to place them first and then work everything else around them as necessary.

The sinks and vanity cabinet are next in order of size, and you usually work with these items next. The sink is the most often used fixture in the bathroom. You should place it near the door, out of the flow of the room's traffic. Work with the toilet location next, which you should locate away from the door for maximum privacy. If your bathroom will include a bidet, place it at the same time as the toilet, and right next to it on the same wall.

If space permits, the use of half-height and full-height walls to separate some or all of the room's usage areas will organize the space neatly, improve the traffic patterns, and increase privacy. Installing doors in these compartment walls will increase privacy even further, and will allow more than one person to use the room at a time. If there is not adequate clearance for a door to swing, whether it's the main access door or a door in one of the compartment walls, you might consider bifold or accordion doors, or a pocket door, which slides into a frame recessed in the wall cavity.

Do not lose sight of your overall goals as you work with the plan. If you need two sinks, plan for them. If you want an exercise area that houses specific pieces of equipment, find a way to fit them in. This planning is where all of your list making pays off. You know exactly what you want and need in this bathroom, and you can play with the designs until everything fits the way you'd like.

Do not get discouraged if the first layouts you try do not work. Professional designers try a number of layouts before they capture the right one for the room, so keep experimenting. Try different types of doors and different vanity cabinets. If necessary, substitute smaller fixtures to gain space. Here is where a complete manufacturer's catalog will be a big help. Fixtures are available in a variety of sizes (see Chapter 4), and sometimes a fixture that is just a few inches smaller will be enough to make a big difference in your layout.

Additional Layout and Design Considerations

As with any remodeling endeavor, large or small, some aspects of the project are more involved than others. Sometimes a major structural or plumbing operation needs to be undertaken, no matter how expensive or complicated, in order to have the bathroom turn out as you'd like. However, having some idea of how involved a particular aspect of the job is can sometimes help you avoid it, thereby saving time, money, and even some frustration.

Moving a sink location a short distance or adding a second sink is relatively minor. Most changes in electrical wiring, although they might involve cutting into the walls and ceiling and then later patching the holes, are also not too involved. Another fairly simple project is adding a new partition wall, since the wall is not load-bearing. In most instances, adding a ventilation fan is pretty straightforward.

Opening up or removing a wall can get quite involved. If the wall is *weight-bearing*, meaning that it carries the weight of rafters, joists, or any load other than itself, great care must be taken in altering it (see Chapter 7). As mentioned earlier, moving plumbing locations sometimes can be a problem, especially if the bathroom has a concrete slab floor.

Another operation that can get tricky is moving a window or door. If the wall is load-bearing, the new opening needs to be properly supported. Also, you have to take the patching of the interior and exterior walls into consideration, in particular matching the siding.

Room additions are another construction project that you should not take too lightly. An addition involves pouring a foundation, framing walls and roof, matching the exterior design and materials, installing a roof, and many other things. Costs can range from moderate to quite expensive, depending on the details of the addition.

Weigh your options carefully as you work on your designs. Initially, let yourself go and experiment with any ideas that occur to you. Then, as things fall into place and your ideas really take shape, try to look at each aspect of the construction process individually and make your decisions accordingly. If you encounter a plumbing or construction detail that seems difficult or expensive, try to find a way of designing around it. If you can't design around it, leave it in and plan your budget and construction schedule accordingly.

BATHROOM DESIGNERS

At some point in the planning stages of your new bathroom, you might wish to consider the services of a professional designer. Most designers who deal with bathrooms have attended a variety of training classes and specialized design seminars, and often can provide the expertise you need to really make a room come together. They can help you with the initial layout of the room, fixture selection and placement, and the overall decorating and color selections for the room.

If your bathroom project is extensive and requires a number of structural changes, you might need the services of a licensed architect. Architects generally have more formal schooling and more advanced structural and engineering training than a designer, but you might need to pay more for their services.

Typically, a designer does not specialize in bathrooms alone because this is simply too small and narrow a field to really keep a designer busy all the time. Kitchen designers usually will do bathrooms also, as will some house designers and some interior decorators. Ask around, and see what areas the designer covers.

Word of mouth is the best recommendation you can get. If you know of anyone who has used a designer in the past and has been satisfied with him, that is a good place to start. You can check with contractors or material suppliers for names, or with your local building department. You can always resort to the Yellow Pages also; if you do not see any listings under "Bathroom," check under "Kitchen."

Your working relationship with a designer is important. You need to find a person who you are comfortable with and who will listen to your needs and ideas. You want guidance and suggestions from a designer, but you do not want someone who will force his styles and design concepts on you.

Arrange an initial interview with the designer at his office, and discuss your needs with him. A short initial meeting is usually free, and gives you both the opportunity to get to know one another. Explain your situation to him, including your own ideas and the budget you have for this project. Ask what type of work he's done in the past, and look at any available photographs of his work. If you have specialized needs, such as for someone who's disabled, find out if the designer has dealt with designs of that sort in the past.

Finally, find out what the fee is, and determine exactly what that fee covers. Some designers are also contractors, and will waive a design fee if you contract with them to do the actual construction. Others charge by the hour or by the complete job. Be certain you know exactly what you will be paying and exactly what you will receive.

If the initial conference goes well and you feel that the designer is competent and you will be comfortable working with him, ask to see some past jobs that are similar to yours. Talk to former clients, and find out if they were satisfied with his work.

After you select the designer for your project, he will need to make at least one visit to your home.

He will carefully examine and measure the bathroom, look over the style and decor of the rest of the home, and perhaps discuss the project with your entire family to get a thorough idea of what you want.

The more input you can provide as to what you are trying to achieve with the room, the better off you will be. Show your designer your job file, including any designs or sketches you have made or photographs you have clipped out and saved. Be as exact as possible about your desires. In this way, you will have a better chance of getting the room you really want, and you will keep the design fees to a minimum.

Sketches will usually come next, in which both of you can try out some ideas and come to a mutual agreement on how the project will look. Finished drawings will be next, and if the job is particularly large, a perspective drawing might be prepared so that you can better visualize the final result.

Some designers are out of the picture at this point, but most will follow up on progress during the construction process and help you solve any problems that arise. This follow-up might include conferring with a contractor, specifying and selecting materials, or even going shopping with him. Once again, you need to determine what services you will be receiving and what you will be charged.

CONTRACTORS AND SUBCONTRACTORS

Whether or not to employ the services of a contractor is another decision you will need to make. As with the decision about a designer, using a contractor is largely dependent on the complexity of the project and your own abilities with a hammer and a pipe wrench.

Evaluating Yourself

Now is the time for a good, honest evaluation of yourself and your abilities. Ask yourself some questions, and be as honest and realistic with your answers as possible:

☐ How much do-it-yourself experience do you have with the various construction trades that will be needed on your project? These areas might include rough and finish carpentry, electrical wiring, plumbing, sheet metal work, roof patching, drywall installation or repair, ceramic tile, painting and wallpapering, and installing flooring.

☐ How involved is your bathroom project? Are there major structural or plumbing changes that you are not comfortable performing yourself?

☐ How much time do you realistically have to devote to the project? Remember that your family will be without the use of the bathroom for much of the time that the work is underway. An experienced contractor might complete the work in a week or two, while you might have to devote a month or more if you are only working on it nights and weekends.

☐ Do you have the necessary tools, or can you buy or rent them?

☐ Are you familiar with the materials you'll need, and do you know where to get them?

☐ Are you comfortable hiring, scheduling, and overseeing the work of others, if you decide to do only part of the work yourself?

Doing your own remodeling can be enjoyable and satisfying, and you can sometimes save a substantial amount of labor costs. Undertaking more than you can handle, however, can end up being a tremendous drain on you physically, as well as on your time, your family, and your patience.

General Contractors

A *general contractor* is someone who is skilled in a variety of construction trades, and is experienced in job management, scheduling, and specification and purchasing of materials. Some general contractors do the work themselves, while others act as an overall coordinator for their own crews and those of their subcontractors.

Selecting and hiring a general contractor is essentially the same as selecting a designer. A word-of-mouth recommendation from a satisfied customer is usually your best way of finding someone reputable. If you know of someone in your neighborhood who is having or has had a bathroom remodeled, even if you do not know them, stop by and introduce

BIANCHINA CONSTRUCTION
Bend, Oregon
Oregon Contractor's License #47104

PROPOSAL and CONTRACT

Date __November 12,_____, 19_8X___

TO ___Mr. & Mrs. Frank Barker_____

_____1204 Century Acres Drive_____

Dear Sir:

____I____ propose to furnish all materials and perform all labor necessary to complete the following: _Remodel existing master bathroom and construct a new half bathroom_ _in existing storage closet off living room. Exact plans and_ _specifications are attached to this contract, and become part of_ _it. Work to commence January 3, 198X, and will be substantially_ _completed by January 30, 198X._

All of the above work to be completed in a substantial and workmanlike manner according to standard practices for the sum of __Thirty one hundred & eighty__ Dollars (xx3,180.00xxx)

Payments to be made ___$500.00 deposit before work begins_____
_____$1,500.00 upon completion of rough plumbing_____
_____$1,180.00 upon final inspections___ as the work progresses
to the value of _____one hundred_____ per cent (_100_ %) of all work completed. The entire amount of contract to be paid within ____fifteen (15)_____ days after completion.

Any alteration or deviation from the above specifications involving extra cost of material or labor will only be executed upon written orders for same, and will become an extra charge over the sum mentioned in this contract. All agreements must be made in writing.

Respectfully submitted,

By ___PB_____
Paul Bianchina, Owner

ACCEPTANCE

You are hereby authorized to furnish all materials and labor required to complete the work mentioned in the above proposal, for which _____we_____ agree to pay the amount mentioned in said proposal, and according to the terms thereof.

ACCEPTED __Frank Barker_____   Mr. Frank Barker_____

Date __11-13_____, 19_8X___

In Pads — AICO-UTILITY Line Form No. 55-037   Spiral Bound — Duplicate — Form No. 50-250

Fig. 3-7. A standard, simplified contract form is used by many contractors. All the details of the job should be spelled out, either in the contract or in an attached specification sheet, and the contract should not contain any blank spaces.

32

yourself. Most people are happy to discuss their remodeling projects, good or bad, and you might get some valuable recommendations. Material suppliers are another good source of recommendations, as is the building department or any subcontractors you might know.

Have the contractor visit your home and examine the project carefully. Provide him with as much information about the project as possible, especially with regard to specific fixtures or other materials you want, and decide exactly which aspects of the project he will perform. If you are getting competitive bids from more than one contractor, which is a good idea, be sure you provide each with the same information so that you can compare the bids accurately.

If possible, examine some of the contractor's finished projects, especially ones that are similar to your own. Talk with the homeowners, and find out as much as you can about the contractor and his work. Did he live up to his contract? Was the job done on time? How was his crew? How were his subcontractors? How well did he respond to changes or problems? These and other questions can tell you a lot about a contractor and what to expect from him.

Subcontractors

If you are comfortable doing some or most of the work yourself, you might wish to act as your own general contractor. In this capacity, you will hire the subcontractors that you need to complete the portions of the job you do not wish to do yourself, such as plumbing or electrical wiring. You will be responsible for scheduling and overseeing the job, and you will need to direct the efforts of your subcontractors and handle any questions or problems that might come up.

This method of handling your remodeling project works well in some instances, especially when only a few subcontractors are involved, and you can save some of the money that would otherwise go to the general contractor for his supervision duties. If the project is large and involved, however, and if you do not have the time to oversee and schedule

it properly, hiring a general contractor to handle the whole thing might be money well spent.

The Contract

If you hire a general contractor, you will be asked to sign a contract. (See Fig. 3-7.) This contract is for the protection of both you and the contractor, and its details need to be mutually agreed upon before it is executed.

Be certain the contract spells out in detail exactly what will be done, what materials will be used, what the estimated dates of commencement and completion are, and what the exact cost will be. If you are doing some of the labor yourself or supplying some of the materials, agree on the specifics with the contractor and have these details included in the contract.

Make sure you understand the details of the contract completely. It should not contain any blank spaces, and you should receive a copy that is identical to the original. Keep a copy of the contract and the job specifications in your job file to refer to as necessary.

BUILDING CODES AND PERMITS

You, and any contractors you use, are obligated to perform the remodeling work on your bathroom according to the specific building, plumbing, and electrical codes in force in your area. These codes are for your safety, and dealing with the building department is not something that you should try to avoid.

If you are altering the structure, plumbing, or wiring, you will probably need a building permit, and it will be up to you or your contractor to obtain it. You will need to provide the building department with a set of plans detailing the project, and they will make periodic inspections of the job as different phases are completed to verify that the work has been done safely and is in compliance with the codes. If you are doing a lot of the work yourself, the building department can be an invaluable source of information. It is also an independent source that will verify the quality of the work your contractor is doing.

Chapter 4

Selecting Fixtures: Toilets and Bidets

IN TERMS OF COST PER SQUARE FOOT, THE BATH-room is the most expensive room in the house to remodel. Within a relatively small space are a number of components, and the largest and most expensive of them are the fixtures. Most bathrooms, regardless of size or style, contain most or all of the same basic fixtures—toilet, sink, bathtub, and shower. It would seem, therefore, that shopping for and selecting these items for your new bathroom would be a fairly easy task, but that's not always the case.

As you begin shopping for fixtures, you will find that you have a bewildering array of choices. Pick up a few manufacturer's catalogs and you will quickly discover hundreds of possibilities—different styles, different sizes, different colors, different features, different efficiencies, and different possible combinations of all four.

You will also find quite a disparity in fixture prices. They can ruin the most carefully planned budget in a real hurry. Even the simple toilet can be found in prices ranging from under $75.00 to well over $500.00, and the toilet seat is extra!

You should begin shopping for fixtures early, before you get too far into the design and especially before you finalize your budget. Visit a well-equipped plumbing store, one with a showroom of fixtures, and spend some time looking over the selection. (See Fig. 4-1.) Pick up some catalogs for future reference, and jot down the prices next to the pictures of the ones in which you are most interested. If the catalog does not list the available fixture sizes, ask a salesperson. Note the sizes in the catalog also. As you finalize your plans you might find that a few inches makes a big difference.

Compare the choices carefully. Remember that you probably will have to live with the fixtures you select day in and day out for many years. You want to be certain that you get attractive, high-quality fixtures that will perform well and last for the life of your new bathroom, but you do not want to pay a lot for features you do not really need. A little shopping around and studying the catalogs usually will narrow the choices rather quickly.

As with many home-improvement items, the price of bathroom fixtures is usually a pretty good indicator of quality. As prices go up, so does durability, efficiency, appearance, and ease of maintenance. Try to purchase the highest quality fixtures you can afford, even at the expense of some of the other items in the bathroom. Inexpensive towel bars and floor coverings can be easily changed later on, but you will be living with the fixtures you choose for many years.

Color choices are another thing you will have to deal with when selecting your fixtures, so you will need to finalize your decorating scheme before making your final decisions. White is the basic, standard color for virtually all fixtures, and carries the lowest price tag. You will almost always pay extra to get a fixture in a color other than white—the amount varies between manufacturers. Some colors require a special order, which might add still more to the fixture's price, and might require 6 weeks or more for delivery. Be sure to verify prices and delivery dates with the salesperson.

When thinking about colors, try to visualize that color fixture in your bathroom five or ten years from now. Times and trends change, and today's ''hot'' color might be out of style in a year or two. Pink and turquoise fixtures, so popular in years past, are now rarely seen in bathrooms, or even in manufac-

turer's catalogs. What seems very much in vogue today, you might absolutely hate tomorrow, and a wildly decorated bathroom might hurt the home's resale value. You do not need to be shackled to white fixtures, but you might want to consider some of the more muted, neutral colors. They will be easier to work around as you redecorate in coming years, and will have a broader appeal should you choose to sell the home in the future.

Once you know what fixtures you want, watch the newspapers for sales. Large plumbing outlets that buy in volume can offer good and sometimes substantial savings, and if there aren't any such outlets locally, it might even be worth a trip out of town to do your shopping. You'll also find occasional sales on fixtures that are in discontinued colors, or that have slight and usually unnoticeable flaws in the finish. Be certain you know why the fixture you are

Fig. 4-1. A small sampling of the many top quality style- and color-coordinated bathroom fixtures now on the market (Courtesy of Universal-Rundle Corporation).

buying has been discounted. If it's flawed, check that the flaw doesn't affect the fixture's operation, and that the manufacturer's warranty is still in effect.

TOILET TYPES

In selecting the right toilet, there are several things to take into consideration. Toilets are available in one- or two-piece designs; in four different flushing actions; in several different styles; in floor-, wall-, or corner-mounted models; and in quite a surprising number of colors. The toilet seat is usually sold separately, and you will find a wide selection of styles and colors in them, also. Just take the choices one at a time and narrow down the field as you go. In this way you are sure to end up with the right one for your needs.

The only choice you won't be faced with is in material. All toilets are constructed from *vitreous china*. This is china that has been exposed to high levels of heat, making it hard, waterproof, and somewhat brittle. Vitreous china is the material of choice because it is sanitary and very resistant to staining, in addition to being very easy to clean. A reasonable amount of care must be taken in handling and installing vitreous china toilets in order to prevent cracking.

Your first and easiest decision will be whether the toilet is to be floor- or wall-mounted. The vast majority of toilets now in use are floor-mounted, and if you are reusing plumbing that is already in the floor, this decision might be made for you. Floor-mounted toilets, being the most popular, offer the greatest range of style, color, and price choices. (See Figs. 4-2 & 4-3.)

If your bathroom is small and space is at a premium, your design might call for a corner toilet, which is also floor-mounted. If so, you will need to know that in advance, since your style and color choices in this type will be limited considerably.

Another possibility is the wall-mounted toilet, whose primary advantage is easier cleaning of the floor under and around the fixture. These, too, are fairly uncommon, and choices might be limited. Wall-mounted toilets require that the plumbing for the soil line be brought up into the wall, and that special rein-

Fig. 4-2. A typical, floor-mounted two-piece toilet (Courtesy of Universal-Rundle Corporation).

forcing within the wall be provided for mounting. (See Fig. 4-4.) If you are selecting a wall-mounted toilet, be sure to get a copy of the installation instructions well in advance, and plan the installation according to the manufacturer's recommendations.

You will be faced next with choices of style and flushing action, as well as whether the toilet is one piece or two. These choices are somewhat interconnected; for example, choosing a particular style of toilet might limit you to a particular flushing action. Base your choices on those elements that are most important to you, and let the other choices fall into line as necessary.

Toilets might be purchased in one-piece or two-piece designs, and the design dictates the style and appearance of the toilet to a great degree. In a two-piece design (Fig. 4-5), the tank and bowl are two separate units, and are assembled on the job before installation with brass bolts and rubber washers.

Fig. 4-3. Another two-piece, floor-mounted toilet. This beautiful recreation, which features an oak seat and brass-plated pipes, offers a top-quality flushing mechanism with the appearance of an old-fashioned wash-down toilet. Rough-in and installation are the same as for a conventional toilet (Courtesy of Kohler Co.).

Two-piece toilets are still the most common, primarily because they are less expensive.

One-piece toilets (Fig. 4-6), have an integral tank and bowl assembly, which results in a considerably lower tank height and a much more sleek and streamlined appearance. This low, clean look suits the style of many of the more modern bathroom decors, and accounts for the increase in popularity in one-piece designs in recent years. They also eliminate the possibility of a leak between the tank and the bowl. You can expect to pay more for a one-piece toilet, with prices ranging from moderately to considerably higher than two-piece models.

Much of your choice in style is dictated by whether the toilet is one- or two-piece. As mentioned previously, two-piece toilets have a higher tank and a bulkier, more "boxy" look, while the one-piece designs are lower and somewhat less obtrusive.

The other choice, which again might be decided for you if you like the style and price of a particular toilet, is the flushing action. There are four basic types of flushing designs, which vary in efficiency and noise level. To some people, the flushing action is the farthest thing from their minds when they shop for a toilet. For others it is an important consideration, especially if they have had a noisy, leaky toilet in the past.

TOILET FLUSHING ACTIONS

The toilet can represent a sizable outlay of money. It is good to know about, and at least consider, the flushing actions when making your selection.

Wash-down Toilets

The wash-down toilet is the oldest, least efficient, and definitely noisiest of the four common toilet flushing actions. Waste is forced from the bowl by the pressure of the water when it is released from the tank, which does not provide a very thorough flushing action. It has a small water area and a small trap, which can increase the possibility of a clog.

The only advantage to toilets of this type is that they are the least expensive of all the designs. Check with your local plumbing inspector before purchasing a wash-down toilet. The current plumbing codes in many area will not allow their use.

Reverse-Trap Toilets

The reverse-trap toilet is probably the most common toilet in use today. It is moderately priced,

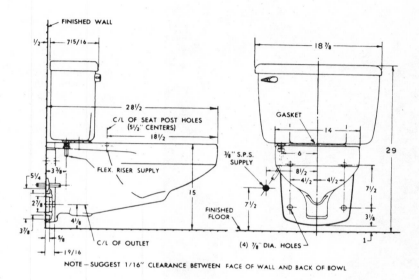

GLENWALL TOILET

2093. SER.

VITREOUS CHINA — CLOSE COUPLED COMBINATION

2093. SERIES ELONGATED
SHOWN WITH
3/8 FLEX. SUPPLY

NOTE — SUGGEST 1/16" CLEARANCE BETWEEN FACE OF WALL AND BACK OF BOWL

NOTE: CARRIER FITTING AS REQUIRED TO BE FIGURED AND FURNISHED BY OTHERS.

DIMENSIONS SHOWN FOR SUPPLY ARE SUGGESTED

NOTE: 3/8" supply pipe not included with toilet and must be ordered separately.

PLUMBER NOTE — Provide suitable reinforcement for all wall supports.

IMPORTANT: Dimensions of fixtures are nominal and may vary within the range of tolerance established by ANSI Standards A112.19.2.

These measurements are subject to change or cancellation. No responsibility is assumed for use of superseded or voided leaflets.

AMERICAN STANDARD

T234

96

MAY, 1982

Fig. 4-4. A wall-hung toilet, which requires a soil line and additional reinforcement in the wall (Courtesy of American Standard).

Fig. 4-5. A modern two-piece toilet with a sleek, rounded design and 3½ gallon, siphon-jet flushing (Courtesy of Kohler Co.).

widely available in several colors, and considerably quieter and more efficient than the wash-down model. It features a larger trap and a larger water surface than the wash-down toilet, and the flushing action through the reverse trap creates a siphoning action to better empty and cleanse the bowl. Also, more of the inside of the bowl is cleansed with water during each flush, making this design more sanitary than the wash-down.

Siphone-Jet Toilets

Next up the line in price, efficiency, and quiet operation is the siphon-jet toilet. This design fea-tures a larger water area, with a greater percent-age of the interior of the bowl being contacted by water during each flush. The trap is also larger with less chance of clogging, and the trap offers a larger seal area. A jet of water starts the flushing cycle, and the siphon action of the trap acts to thoroughly empty the bowl.

Siphon-Action Toilets

Also called *siphon-vortex* toilets, toilets of this design are the best available. The flushing action, which creates a whirlpool effect in the bowl, thoroughly cleans and flushes the interior and leaves virtually no part of the bowl untouched by water. This type of toilet has a very large water surface area, and a large trap area and trap seal. Siphon-action toilets are virtually silent in operation, but they are the most expensive of the toilet designs, and are available in one-piece models only.

WATER CONSERVATION

Water conservation is a growing concern for everyone these days, as increases in population continue to place greater demands on our water supplies. In homes where the water is metered and the homeowner is charged by actual usage, wasting water can have some adverse economic consequences also.

One place to consider the potential for saving water is with the purchase of your toilet. The typical "standard" toilet consumes about 5 to 7 gallons of water per flushing cycle. With many manufacturers now offering water-conserving toilets, you can find many models that reduce that consumption to around 3 to 3½ gallons, and some units have reduced

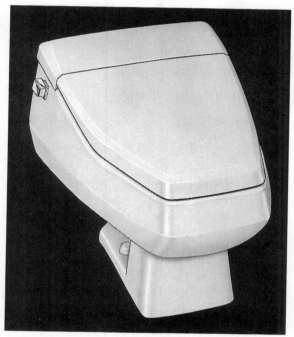

Fig. 4-6. A low-profile, one-piece toilet with a water-saving, virtually silent flushing action (Courtesy of Kohler Co.).

consumption to only 1 gallon or less. For example, Microflush, a leader in the field of low-flow plumbing fixtures, offers a toilet that uses only ½ gallon of water per flush while still maintaining a full-size water surface area for thorough bowl cleaning. (See Fig. 4-7.) This model represents a water-use reduction of as much as 90 percent over conventional toilets.

For a large family with metered water, saving that much water on every use of the toilet can amount to some pretty substantial savings over the years. In addition, state-of-the-art water-conserving toilets can reduce the amount of ground absorption area required for a septic system by as much as 40 percent. Toilets of this type are sometimes the only answer in areas where sewer or water limitations have created a moratorium on further residential or commercial building development.

In addition to toilets that are actually designed to conserve water, there are also dams and other devices on the market that can reduce the amount of water used by standard toilets. Many of these devices will work fine in most types of toilets, with no adverse effects. In some cases, however, the reduced water flow affects the flushing cycle and the efficiency of the toilet. Before installing any water-saving device in a new or existing toilet, it is best to check with the toilet manufacturer or your local plumbing supply dealer for specific instructions and recommendations.

SPECIAL-USE TOILETS

The most common type of special-use toilet is the *safety toilet*, which you will want to consider if you are planning your bathroom with an elderly or disabled person in mind. Toilets of this type have a more elongated seat design, and the seat is 18 inches off the floor instead of the 14-inch height found on conventional toilets. True safety toilets also have sturdy grab bars mounted alongside the seat, although you can substitute wall-mounted grab bars if desired. Once again, style and color choices are limited, and you will probably need to place a special order, so plan accordingly.

If you are planning a new bathroom in a below-grade area such as a basement, where the flow of the waste materials would need to be uphill in order to connect with the home's soil lines, installing a toilet can present some difficulties. One solution is the *up-flush toilet*. When flushed, this type of toilet uses a strong jet of water to break up solids, followed by a second water jet that forces the liquefied waste up a pipe and into the overhead soil lines. Maximum lift is about 10 feet at 40 pounds per square inch of water pressure.

Another possibility for basements, or for any place where access to water and soil lines is a problem or where ecological considerations are of primary importance, is the *composting toilet*. (See Fig. 4-8.) Composting toilets require no water or soil line

connections, and can be installed just about anywhere in less than an hour. In fact, the only connections are for the vent pipes, which vent the unit to the outside.

As much as 90 percent of the material entering the toilet is water. Composting toilets work by first evaporating most of that water through a specially designed aeration system. The remaining waste material is transformed into dry, clean soil through the actions of the toilet's built-in warm air system and the natural process of organic material breakdown called *composting*, the same process that takes place in your garden compost pile. Every 3 to 6 months (the actual time span is dependent on how much use

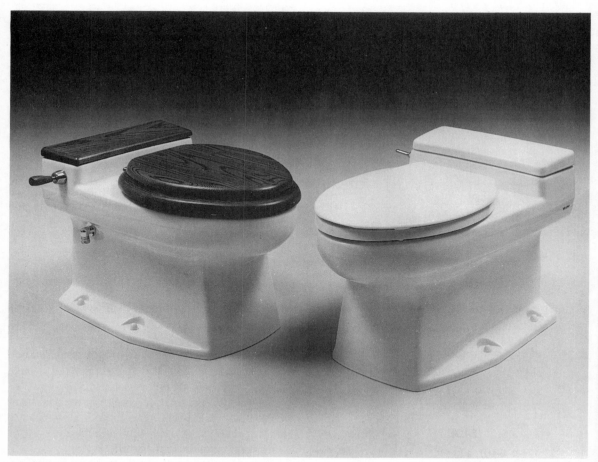

Fig. 4-7. Two examples of high-quality, water-saving toilets. Each of these toilets uses only ½ gallon of water per flushing cycle (Courtesy of Microphor).

Fig. 4-8. A composting toilet, which can be installed with no water or soil lines. The only connection is the vertical vent pipe, which is attached to the top of the toilet and vents it to the outside (Courtesy of Sancor Industries Ltd.).

the toilet gets), a tray containing environmentally clean soil residue is removed from the bottom of the toilet for disposal. (See Fig. 4-9.)

Composting toilets are not cheap. Their price tag is about two to five times that of a top-quality conventional toilet, and their appearance is not always an interior decorator's dream. They're a simple project for the do-it-yourselfer, however, and the reduced installation costs, especially for remodeling and vacation home situations, can help offset some of the initial purchase price. The typical composting toilet will handle the needs of an average family of five, and offers the added advantage of having a very positive impact on the environment.

BIDETS

The bidet (Fig. 4-10), a fairly common fixture in European bathrooms but until recently rarely seen anywhere else, has enjoyed a substantial increase in popularity in the United States in the last several years. It is still considered something of a ''luxury'' fixture, although it doesn't need to add substantially to the room's cost if planned and budgeted for initially. It is a fixture that is almost always found only in the master bathroom.

The bidet is a personal hygiene fixture, and has an appearance similar to that of a toilet. Hot and cold water faucets, either bowl- or wall-mounted, control the water temperature and water pressure. The user sits on the bidet facing the back wall (backward from the way a toilet is used), and a spray of warm water is used to wash the pelvic and anal areas. A bowl flushing action is usually incorporated into the design to help keep the bowl clean, and many models also include a bowl stopper so that the bidet can be used as a foot bath or even for washing clothes.

Although the bidet can be located in its own private area of the bath, most designs place it directly

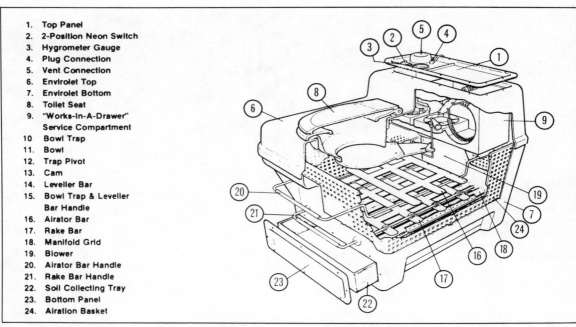

1. Top Panel
2. 2-Position Neon Switch
3. Hygrometer Gauge
4. Plug Connection
5. Vent Connection
6. Envirolet Top
7. Envirolet Bottom
8. Toilet Seat
9. "Works-In-A-Drawer" Service Compartment
10. Bowl Trap
11. Bowl
12. Trap Pivot
13. Cam
14. Leveller Bar
15. Bowl Trap & Leveller Bar Handle
16. Airator Bar
17. Rake Bar
18. Manifold Grid
19. Blower
20. Airator Bar Handle
21. Rake Bar Handle
22. Soil Collecting Tray
23. Bottom Panel
24. Airation Basket

Fig. 4-9. The inner workings of the composting toilet. Dry soil, the result of the composting process, is collected in the tray at the bottom for later disposal (Courtesy of Sancor Industries, Ltd.).

Fig. 4-10. A modern bidet, with deck-mounted faucet and pop-up stopper assembly. The bidet's sleek design matches that of the toilet in Figure 4-5, and is typical of the matching toilet/bidet combinations offered by many manufacturers (Courtesy of Kohler Co.).

Fig. 4-11. Another example of today's design- and color-coordinated styling is shown here in this contemporary, carefully-matched toilet, bidet and pedestal sink set (Courtesy of American Standard).

beside the toilet. In this manner, the drain and vent lines of the two fixtures can be tied together, and plumbing of the water lines is simplified. (The bidet requires a hot water line.) If you purchase a bidet from the same manufacturer as the toilet you are using, you will usually find both fixtures in many of the same colors and styles. (See Fig. 4-11.)

The dimensions of the bidet are very similar to those of a toilet (Fig. 4-12), another feature that makes the two compatible for placement side by side. Plan on allowing the same side and front clearances as you would for a toilet.

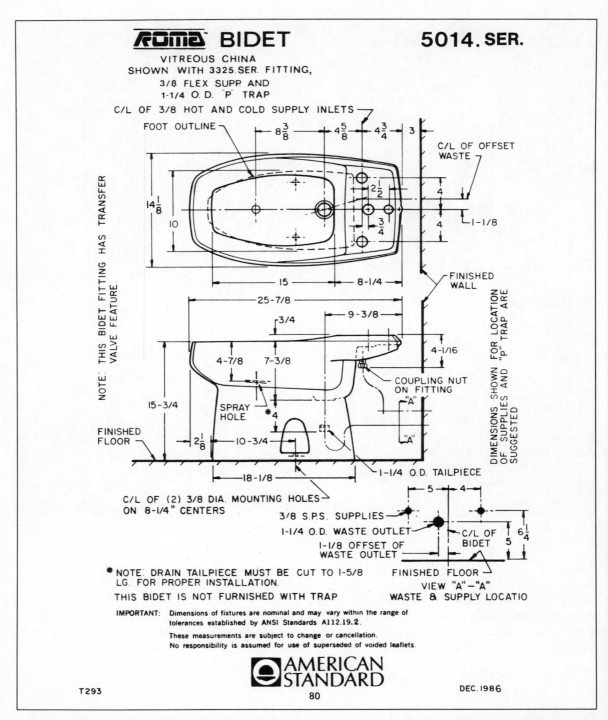

Fig. 4-12. The dimensions and plumbing connection layout shown here are typical of most bidets, and are similar to the overall size of many toilets (Courtesy of American Standard).

Chapter 5

Selecting Fixtures: Bathtubs, Showers, Sinks, and Faucets

YOUR CHOICES ABOUND WHEN IT COMES TIME TO make selections for the other fixtures in your bathroom. A rainbow of colors, plus literally hundreds of shapes, styles, combinations, and configurations make shopping fun and exciting, and perhaps a little confusing. Do not get discouraged when the selections seem a little overwhelming; stick to the decisions and designs you formulated in your planning and list-making sessions; keep your overall color scheme and "look" in mind (and your budget) and the decisions will become surprisingly easy.

MATERIALS

In the process of selecting your new toilet, the one decision you didn't have to make was selecting the material with which it was made. As you move on to choose your bathtub, shower, and sinks, material choice becomes just as important as size, shape, and color in designing a bathroom with which you will be happy.

You might find it easier to make a decision if you know more about your choice of materials. Each material offers certain advantages and disadvantages; not all types and sizes of units are available in all materials.

Fiberglass

Bathtubs, showers, shower pans, and sinks made of fiberglass are a very popular choice today. *Fiberglass* is a catch-all word. It is typically used to describe a polyester resin material reinforced with chopped glass fibers, but acrylics are usually lumped into this group also.

The fiberglass molding process allows the material to be shaped easily and inexpensively into a wide variety of configurations. You will find many units with convenient seats, grab bars, soap dishes, shampoo shelves, and other features molded in.

Another definite advantage to this molding process is the creation of the one-piece tub/shower combination. The shower walls and tub base are continuous and seamless, which eliminates cracks and joints, ensures water-tightness, and makes the fixtures easier to clean. Fiberglass units are light and easy to handle, attractively styled to fit a number of decors, and moderately priced. They are warm to the touch, fairly quiet, and available in several colors.

Fiberglass has some disadvantages, too. Early units had a relatively thin gel-coat finish that was easily chipped and scratched, and that dulled with time. Newer finishing techniques have refined and thickened the coating process, however, and have greatly improved these drawbacks. Fiberglass fixtures require a little more care, and must be cleaned with a nonabrasive cleaner. Some units are rather flimsy, and might require additional backing to prevent distortion or cracking. Also, fiberglass does not keep water hot, so the units should be insulated well upon installation. For some people, appearance might be an additional drawback to fiberglass. Most fiberglass fixtures lack the color depth and richness of cast iron, and their sleeker, more modern styling might not be right for all decorating motifs.

Currently, fiberglass is the most popular material on the market, so the choices are quite wide. Do some objective shopping and carefully compare the quality of construction and finish of the various fiberglass units, and also of the fixtures made of fiberglass vs. those made of other materials.

Cast Iron

The cast-iron bathtub dates back to the late 1800s, and for many years, cast iron was the "standard" material used in the construction of residential bathtubs. It is still a popular material today, particularly for sinks, although its use in bathtubs has declined. Cast-iron showers are not available.

After being cast to the shape of the bathtub, the iron is coated with a baked-on enamel that is relatively thick (about $1/16$ inch), resulting in a finish that is rich, strong, and glossy. Cast-iron tubs and sinks are virtually indestructible in normal use, and the enamel is strong, durable, and very resistant to chipping.

A number of color choices are available, and the color has a very deep, rich sheen to it that is very attractive. Cast-iron tubs also have the added, although often overlooked, advantages of being very quiet and keeping the bath water hot longer.

Cast iron is thick and heavy; a standard tub weighs in between 300 and 400 pounds. Even the larger sinks can weigh close to 100 pounds. The weight factor adds to the shipping costs and makes cast-iron tubs hard to handle, especially in a remodeling situation. In some instances the floor framing might need to be reinforced to handle the additional weight. Cast-iron units are also expensive compared to some other materials.

Enameled Steel

Enameled steel tubs and sinks are similar to cast-iron units in some ways. The steel is first shaped, then coated with a layer of baked-on enamel. The enamel coating is usually a little thinner, however, and is more susceptible to damage from chipping. Enameled steel fixtures are available in several colors, but most people find that the color layer lacks the richness of cast-iron fixtures.

The steel, because of its greater strength, is thinner than the cast iron, making it lighter (about 100 pounds for a standard bathtub) and easier to handle—a real plus in remodeling situations. Steel tubs are noisier than cast iron and less able to keep water hot, although many manufacturers offer an undercoating that helps with both problems. Most enameled steel fixtures are priced moderately.

Ceramic Tile

Ceramic tile has been a popular choice in bathrooms throughout history, and is still widely used today. There are thousands of color, pattern, texture, size, and shape combinations available. Finding something that suits your tastes and decor is virtually assured. Tiles are available imprinted with paintings of flowers, wildlife, ships, abstract designs, and many other decorative items. Some are designed to fit together into prearranged patterns to create very striking murals. In addition to the stock choices available, you also can have custom tiles created in any look or pattern you wish, many at a surprisingly reasonable cost.

Ceramic tile is a "custom" material, in that you cannot buy an actual tub or shower that is already tiled and ready for installation. A shape for the tub or shower is created first, protected with a waterproof covering material, then tiled. (See Fig. 5-1.) This process creates individualized tub and shower shapes and sizes, and has the definite advantage of solving the problems associated with fitting a "standard" size fixture into some of the odd spaces created by remodeling.

Ceramic tile is rich and beautiful, lends itself to any decor, and has an elegance and individuality that is attractive to just about everyone. It is strong, long-lasting, noise-deadening, and, although initially

Fig. 5-1. For a mortar-base tile installation, the preferred method of tiling a tub or shower, metal lath is first applied to the walls as a backing for the mortar (top). The pan in this shower was formed from a special neoprene sheet (center), then the mortar and tile were applied to the walls. The mortar for the shower pan (bottom) is carefully sloped to the drain in the center, then the tile is applied.

cool to the touch, keeps bath water hot for quite awhile.

Ceramic tile has its disadvantages, too. Most tub and shower applications require professional installation, and are fairly expensive. The grout lines between the tiles are subject to mildew and stains, and require more upkeep than other materials. Also, the tile is heavy, particularly over a mortar base, and is subject to cracking under sharp impact. Glazed tile is slippery when wet. Do not use it for tub and shower bottoms unless you provide additional non-skid protection.

Corian

A DuPont product, Corian is an acrylic-based material that somewhat resembles marble. One-piece Corian sink/vanity top combinations are available, (Fig. 5-2), and Corian also is produced in large sheets of varying thicknesses for on-site cutting to produce custom tubs and showers. (See Figs. 5-3 and 5-4.) Corian is a very strong, durable material with a nice richness to it. The color is blended through the entire piece, and scars or burns in the surface can be removed easily with fine sandpaper.

One of the drawbacks to Corian is its price; a custom Corian shower typically will run about twice as much as a comparable custom ceramic tile installation. Colors are limited to white and a few off-white blends. It has a smooth, somewhat glossy surface that blends well with a number of design motifs, although it might appear a little too "institutional" for some tastes.

Corian is also quite heavy, and while the premade sinks and vanity tops are easy to install, cutting and installing the sheet material might prove difficult and time-consuming for the do-it-yourselfer. Precut Corian shower wall and bathtub wall kits also are available to simplify installation.

Simulated Marble and Onyx

A blend of polyester resin, catalyst, fillers, and pigments, simulated marble and onyx materials are cast into bathtubs, shower pans, shower and tub surrounds, and one-piece, seamless sink/vanity top combinations. This man-made material has been refined and improved over the years to create a look that very closely resembles natural marble and onyx at a fraction of the cost of the real quarried material. The material has a traditional rich and elegant appearance, and will blend nicely with modern bathrooms or turn-of-the-century reproductions. It is reasonably strong and durable, is available in a number of colors and color blends, and is moderately priced.

Standard Integral Top and Bowl Sizes

Sizes Single Bowl Inches	mm	Bowl Position* Inches	mm
17" x 19"	430 x 480	C	
17" x 21"	430 x 530	C	
17" x 25"	430 x 630	C	
19½" x 25"	500 x 630	C	
19½" x 31"	500 x 790	C	
19½" x 37"	500 x 940	C	
22" x 25"	560 x 630	C	
22" x 31"	560 x 790	C	
22" x 37"	560 x 940	C	
22" x 43"	560 x 1090	C	
22" x 49"	560 x 1240	15"—LCR—15"	380
22" x 61"	560 x 1550	15"—LCR—15"	380
22" x 67"	560 x 1700	15"—LCR—15"	380
22" x 73"	560 x 1850	18"—LCR—18"	460
22" x 85"	560 x 2100	18"—LCR—18"	460
22" x 102"	560 x 2590	24"—LCR—24"	610
Double Bowl			
22" x 49"	560 x 1240	12½"—LR—12½"	320
22" x 61"	560 x 1550	15½"—LR—15½"	390
22" x 73"	560 x 1850	18½"—LR—18½"	470
22" x 85"	560 x 2160	18½"—LR—18½"	470
22" x 102"	560 x 2590	27"—LR—27"	680
Banjo Style			
61"	560 x 1550	12½"—LR—12½"	320
Corner Bowl		No Backsplash	
24" x 24"	615 x 615	C	

*C-Center, L-Left, R-Right. For non-centered bowls, bowl positions are shown in inches from edge to top to center of drain. Note: Please contact Du Pont where minimum tolerance(s) is critical.

Fig. 5-2. An example of some of the preformed Corian sink and countertop sizes and styles (Courtesy of DuPont).

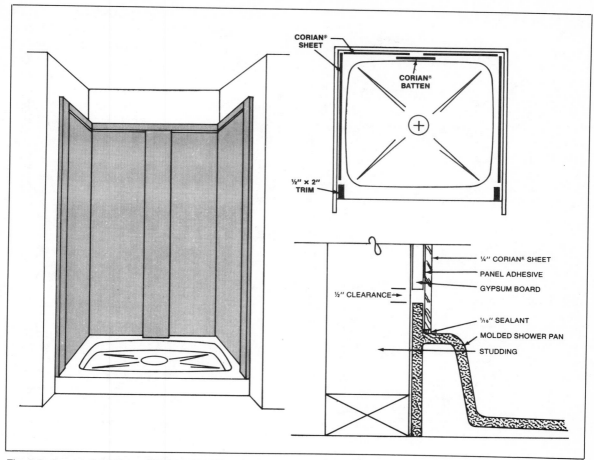

Fig. 5-3. One method for installing Corian sheets with a preformed fiberglass pan to create a custom stall shower. The Corian is put up in four large pieces to simplify installation and correct out-of-plumb walls, then is finished off with three trim pieces (Courtesy of DuPont).

Simulated marble and simulated onyx are fairly heavy, and the sheet materials are probably not for a do-it-yourselfer who has not worked with them before. Cleaning must be done with a nonabrasive cleaner, and some materials are subject to staining, *crazing* (a number of fine lines that appear in the surface), and scratching over time. Be sure to look at a large sample of the material before ordering to be certain the style and color are right for the type room you are trying to create.

Other Materials

A variety of other, less common materials also are used in the creation of premanufactured and custom-built bathroom fixtures, including wood, glazed ceramics, natural marble, hammered copper, and several others. Unusual materials such as these can make your bathroom unique and special, but there are some trade-offs.

Many of these items are ''one-of-a-kind'' and are correspondingly expensive, and ordering times might range from several weeks to several months. Special plumbing parts or other materials might be required, and the actual installation might be beyond the scope of the average do-it-yourselfer. Also, special and perhaps time-consuming cleaning and maintenance procedures might be required. Shop for any unusual material carefully and get all the facts be-

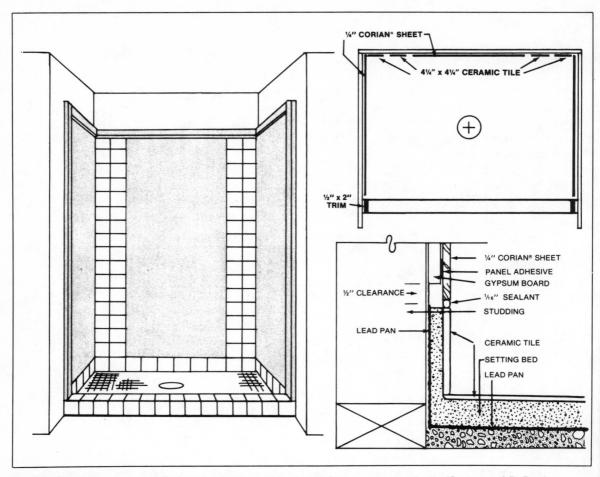

Fig. 5-4. Creating a custom stall shower using a combination of Corian and ceramic tile (Courtesy of DuPont).

fore you make a decision. Be sure you inquire about installation procedures, maintenance, durability, delivery times, shipping costs, and "hidden" costs for necessary extras.

BATHTUBS AND SHOWERS

Bathtubs and showers represent another area of fixture selection where the choices of sizes, styles, colors, and materials are incredibly wide, and equally confusing. Add to that the possibilities of creating a custom-designed, custom-built tub or shower of your own, and the options can become bewildering.

The first and most obvious choice is whether you want a bathtub, a stall shower, or a combination unit. You made this choice when you finalized the bathroom plans. Beyond that, there is no real "best choice" for your new bathroom.

Prefabricated tub, shower, and tub/shower units are the most common choice because of lower cost and faster and easier installation, particularly for the do-it-yourselfer. Custom tubs and showers, on the other hand, offer an unlimited number of size, style, and decorating options. Also, the custom installation sometimes offers the only solution to effectively using an oddly sized or unusually shaped area. Many of the following tub designs also are available in whirlpool models, which are discussed in Chapter 6.

As with all the options you will be considering during the planning and construction of your new bathroom, weigh the possibilities carefully, then make your best selection based on features, appearance, and, as always, your budget.

BATHTUB TYPES AND SIZES

For most people who grew up with the standard rectangular bathtub, it might seem strange to think about bathtub types. However, with the move to increased size and comfort in today's bathrooms, along with a new awareness of creating a pleasant look and a relaxing environment, many new shapes and styles are available. Although the rectangular tub is still the most common, there are some options worth exploring.

Rectangular

For many years, the standard bathtub was 5 feet long and 2½ feet wide. (See Fig. 5-5.) These tubs are still very popular today, both in new designs and remodeling designs, and quite often you will be limited to using this conventional size to replace an existing tub. Sticking with the same size unit as the one you are replacing can save you a number of headaches by eliminating major structural and plumbing alterations.

If you have the design flexibility, however, there are more comfortable sizes available in rectangular tubs. Perhaps the most common alternate size

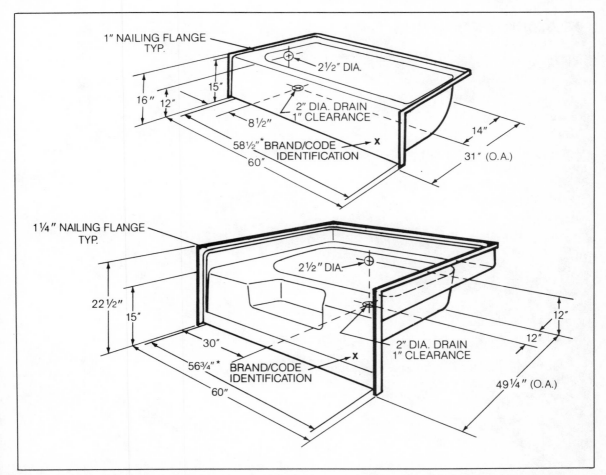

Fig. 5-5. A typical rectangular bathtub (top), and a wider tub with step (bottom) that will fit in the same 5-foot-wide space (Courtesy of Philips Industries).

choice is the 6-foot tub, a length that provides more comfortable and relaxing bathing. Tubs with greater widths are available that are ideal for use by two people, or for bathing two children at the same time. Also, you might want to consider "steeping" or "soaking" tubs with up to 6 inches of greater depth. Remember, with any larger tub, you might need larger pipes and faucets, and perhaps additional water heating capacity.

Rectangular tubs usually are supplied with three open sides and one finished side, for recessing between three walls. Left and right corner models are available that have two finished sides, and some manufacturers also offer models with three finished sides for placement against one wall only. When ordering a tub with one or more finished sides, it's important to specify if you want it left-hand, right-hand, or center-draining, indicating where in the tub the drain outlet hole will be located. The drain location is especially important if you are matching existing plumbing.

Recessed (Sunken or Platform)

Many rectangular tubs also are available for recessing. (See Fig. 5-6.) Recessed tubs have a fin-

Fig. 5-6. A rectangular bathtub with no side panels, designed for recessing into the floor or, as shown here, into a raised platform (Courtesy of Kohler Co.).

54

ished, rounded-over top but no finished sides, and are designed to be set into a raised platform or a cutout in the floor. The tub is reversible in the opening, and does not need to be specified as left- or right-hand.

The recessed look is clean and uncluttered, and elimination of the one exposed side deemphasizes the bulk of the tub and allows you greater decorating freedom. If you choose the raised platform method of installation (Fig. 5-7), you can adapt a recessed tub to almost any remodeling situation and is easy for the do-it-yourselfer. The true *sunken* tub (Fig. 5-8), recessed into the floor, requires additional floor framing and bracing to carry the tub's weight, and usually cannot be done on a second floor without extensive alterations to the framing.

Oval

The oval bathtub (Fig. 5-9), is a variation of the standard rectangular tub, and is becoming increasingly popular. The basic overall size for most of these units is still 5 × 2 ½ feet, making them adaptable to many remodeling situations. Most common is the recessed oval, with a rectangular or oval top and no finished sides. Models with one finished side are also available, however.

Square and Receptor

Square tubs are designed for use in areas where space is limited, and they also work very well as children's tubs. Sizes range from approximately 30 inches to around 50 inches square. Some "square" tubs are actually a little longer on one side than on the other.

Square tubs are available in many different styles, including a square outer shape with a square inner recess, a square outer shape with a rectangular inner recess, no finished sides for use as a recessed tub, and one or more finished sides for use against one or more walls.

A *receptor tub* is essentially a square tub having a shallower depth, usually only 12 inches. These tubs are good choices for bathing small children because access over the low sides is more convenient. They also work well as a base for a shower.

Corner

Another possibility where space is limited is the corner tub. This type tub configuration has an oval or rectangular inner recess with an outer shape that is square on two sides and angled across the front. It is designed for placement in a corner where two walls meet at 90 degrees. The angled front does not

Fig. 5-7. A rectangular whirlpool tub installed in a custom tiled platform.

protrude into the room as far as the rectangular tub, requiring less floor space.

Claw-Foot

A popular fixture for re-creating a "turn-of-the-century" look is the freestanding claw-foot bathtub. You might be able to locate an authentic antique claw-foot tub at antique dealers, and refinish it. Another option is Kohler's modern recreation, a freestanding tub that rests on four brass-plated feet and has a flowing, high-backed shape, reminiscent of the old portable tubs.

Tubs of this type are not designed to be placed directly against the walls, so you cannot conceal the plumbing in the wall recesses. As a result, you will need to use exposed water and waste lines, which should be brass or chrome plated for best appearance. Kohler offers a complete pipe, faucet, and waste combination for use with its tub.

SHOWER TYPES AND SIZES

You can purchase showers as separate stall units (Fig. 5-10), or in combination with a bathtub. (Fig. 5-11). You can also create them by enclosing the walls surrounding a bathtub or shower pan with any variety of waterproof materials. Many sizes and styles of shower stalls and wall panels are available,

Fig. 5-8. A square whirlpool bathtub that has been recessed into the floor. Note the open towel storage (top left) and the open book and curio shelves (top right) (Courtesy of American Standard).

Fig. 5-9. An oval tub in a raised, tiled platform (Courtesy of American Standard).

with colors and patterns designed to match or complement any bathroom decor.

Prefabricated Combination Bathtub/Showers

The demand for the prefabricated fiberglass combination tub/shower has increased tremendously in recent years. Its combination of sleek styling, convenient built-ins, seamless construction, low cost, and easy installation offers something for everyone.

Several sizes are available, with 5 feet wide × 2½ feet deep × 7 feet high being about the most common. (See Fig. 5-12). You will need to specify

Fig. 5-10. A preformed, one-piece fiberglass shower stall (Courtesy of Glastec).

a left- or right-hand waste outlet for the tub. You will drill the end wall panel on the site for whatever shower faucet you are using.

One thing you should remember when shopping for a tub/shower combination to be used in a remodeling situation is whether or not you can get it into the room! This thought might seem obvious, but is often overlooked by remodelers. You can put most units of this type into place only when most of the room's framing is open. These combination units require access through an open exterior wall or through double or patio doors to get it into the house. Some units (Figs. 5-13 and 5-14), have the bathtub and shower surrounds in two pieces for easier movement.

Prefabricated Bathtub Surrounds

Another possibility for dressing up a combination tub/shower, or for creating a new one, is to use prefabricated bathtub surround kits. A number of kits are available, and the sizes, colors, patterns, and built-ins will vary. They all are basically alike in what they do and how they are installed.

The typical kit contains five panels, several tubes of adhesive, color-coordinated caulking, and matching trim panels. The majority of the kits are designed for use with a standard 5- × -2½-foot rectangular tub, but other sizes also are available.

Installation is quick and easy in most cases (Fig. 5-15), consisting of applying adhesive to the backs of the corner panels and putting them in place, followed by the back panel and one end panel. You measure and drill the other end panel as necessary for the tub and shower controls, then apply it to the wall. You should apply the trim pieces last, if used, then you should caulk the entire unit to the tub, the walls, and itself. Since the individual sections overlap each other, adjustments of several inches are possible. This overlapped area allows you to neatly fill the entire wall area, and to adjust to out-of-square walls and other common problems.

Prefabricated Stall Showers

A *prefabricated stall shower* is a three-sided fiberglass unit with a bottom (Fig. 5-16), intended

Fig. 5-11. A fiberglass bathtub/shower combination. Note how the unit was formed to create a headrest at the left side of the tub and a recess for shampoo, soap, and washcloth along the back wall (Courtesy of Universal-Rundle Corporation).

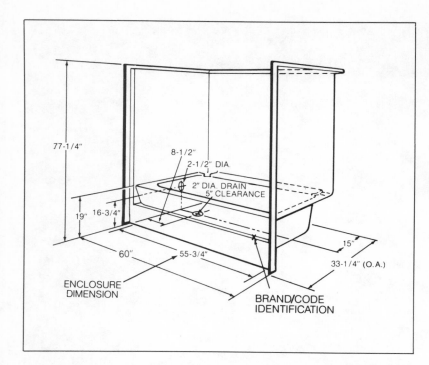

Fig. 5-12. Dimensions of a typical bathtub/shower combination unit (Courtesy of Philips Industries).

for showering only. Sizes range from around 30 × 30 inches up to 36 × 54 inches or larger. (See Fig. 5-17.) The one-piece units are the most common. They are attractive, seamless, and easy to install, but offer many of the same problems of getting them into the room that the tub/shower combination units offer. For remodeling situations, stall showers also are available in two-, three-, or four-piece units that are assembled on-site. (See Figs. 5-17, 5-18, and 5-19.)

You will find a wide variety of styles and colors available, with surface textures that range from totally smooth to a pattern that closely resembles individual tiles. Almost all fiberglass shower stalls come complete with handy shelves, soap dishes, and other convenient and helpful built-ins. Many of the larger units also feature built-in seats.

Some companies still offer prefabricated shower stalls of enameled steel. These stalls typically consist of a floor unit and three wall panels, which are installed individually and overlapped and sealed for water-tightness. These enameled steel units have basically the same advantages and disadvantages as enameled steel bathtubs.

Shower Pans

A *shower pan*, also called a receptor pan, is a square or rectangular pan about 4 inches deep, with a drain hole in the middle. The pan is set on the floor and leveled, then secured through a flange to the wall. You install a wall covering of fiberglass, ceramic tile, or other waterproof material next, overlapping the flange of the shower pan to form a watertight seal.

You can purchase shower pans in several sizes to suit the available space, ranging from 30-×-30-inch to 4- and 5-foot models. Fiberglass is the most common shower pan material, but acrylic, terrazzo, and enameled steel models are available also. Most of these models have a patterned, nonskid surface texture, which is a good feature.

CUSTOM BATHTUBS AND SHOWERS

As mentioned previously, the use of ceramic tile, Corian, synthetic marble, and other materials has made custom tubs and showers of any size and shape available. Such installations require careful

Fig. 5-13. A two-piece bathtub/shower combination, with the bathtub and the shower surrounds installed separately (Courtesy of Glastec).

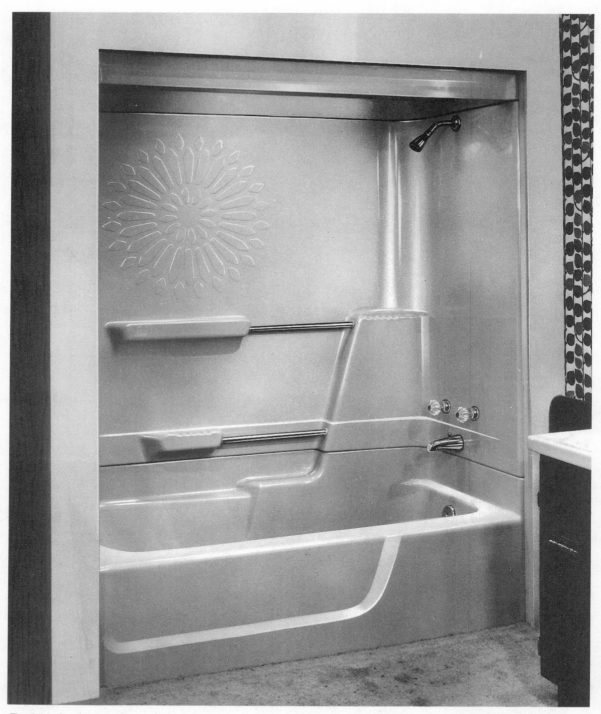

Fig. 5-14. Another two-piece unit, featuring integral grab bars and a molded-in design on the back wall (Courtesy of Universal-Rundle Corporation).

Fig. 5-15. The three stages involved in installing a typical tub surround kit. The corner units
are installed first (top), followed by the back
panel (center) and the two side panels (bottom).
The panels are installed with a waterproof adhesive that's supplied with the kit, then carefully
caulked.

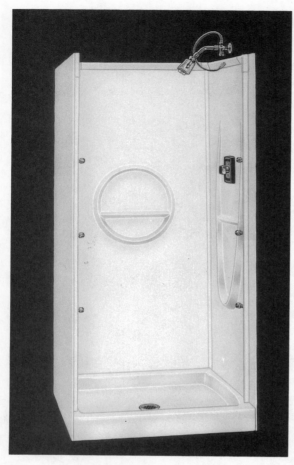

Fig. 5-16. A prefabricated stall shower unit. This model has six spray heads along the front edge, three on each side, in addition to the regular shower head (Courtesy of Kohler Co.).

have completed the enclosure framing, you should create a solid subsurface by installing a plywood facing over the framing, or by placing solid lumber blocking between the studs. You then cover this surface with several alternating layers of asphalt-impregnated felt paper and hot tar, just like a hot-tar roof coating. You should use special two-piece "Roman tub" drains (Fig. 5-1), and seal them into the tar. In some cities, you will find companies that specialize in hot tar tub and shower enclosures, and sometimes roofers will install them as a sideline.

You should apply Corian and other sheet materials directly over the enclosure with adhesive. You can install ceramic tile over a mortar base, which is the traditional and most durable method, or you can apply them directly over the enclosure material with waterproof mastic. (See Fig. 5-20.)

SINKS

There are lots of sizes, shapes, colors, and materials from which to choose when selecting a sink. (See Figs. 5-21 through 5-23.) Visiting a well-equipped plumbing showroom or going through a collection of catalogs usually will be enough to point you in the right direction. The basic types are listed here.

Self-Rimming

The most common type sink is the self-rimming (Fig. 5-24), which has a thick, rounded edge that overlaps the countertop and is supported by it. Sinks of this type are easy to install with adhesive caulking, offer the widest selection of styles and sizes, and will work with any countertop material.

Unrimmed or Under-the-Counter

An unrimmed sink mounts lower than the countertop material. Usually you will clip it to the plywood decking on top the cabinets. You then place the top over the sink, giving it a recessed appearance. These sinks typically do not have faucet holes. You mount the faucet to the countertop instead.

Flush-Mount

A flush-mounted sink is designed for use with a plastic laminate countertop, and is held in place with

waterproofing of the underlying framing before application of the finish materials, and are best left to professional installers.

You might be able to construct a shower using a standard shower pan if one of the appropriate dimensions is available. If not, you can create the pan through the use of special neoprene rubber sheets, lead, copper, or hot tar. You can create waterproof enclosures for custom tubs in the same way.

You can create one of the simplest and least expensive custom enclosures with hot tar. After you

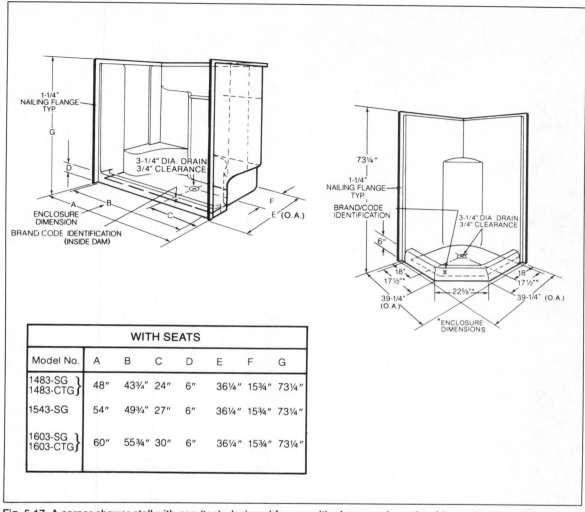

WITH SEATS						
Model No.	A	B	C	D	E	F	G
1483-SG 1483-CTG	48″	43¾″	24″	6″	36¼″	15¾″	73¼″
1543-SG	54″	49¾″	27″	6″	36¼″	15¾″	73¼″
1603-SG 1603-CTG	60″	55¾″	30″	6″	36¼″	15¾″	73¼″

Fig. 5-17. A corner shower stall with pan (top), designed for use with glass panels on the sides and a glass door across the angled front. Units such as these save valuable floor space since they don't require the framed and drywalled enclosure walls that the larger, one-piece stall (bottom) would need (Courtesy of Philips Industries Inc.).

a chrome ring that is screwed on from underneath with special clips. Sinks of this type have lost popularity, owing to the somewhat "cluttered" look of the sink rim and the difficulty of keeping the joint between the rim and the counter clean.

Sink/Counter Combinations

You can achieve a clean, seamless appearance through the use of sink/counter combinations.

Manufacturers construct these combinations using synthetic marble. They cast the sink at the same time they form the counter.

Wall-Hung

If you are not using a vanity cabinet, you can use a sink that is hung on the wall instead. (Fig. 5-25). You mount heavy steel brackets to the studs, then hang the sink from the bracket. Larger units

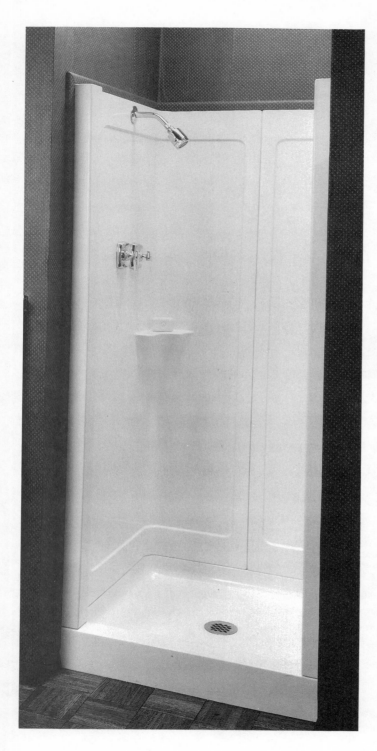

Fig. 5-18. A three-piece stall shower. The molded pan is installed first, followed by the two side panels (Courtesy of Glastec).

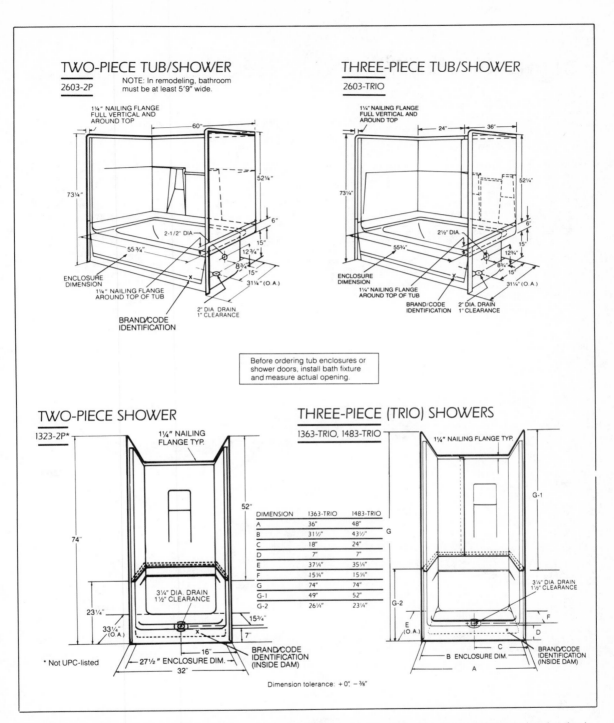

TWO-PIECE TUB/SHOWER

2603-2P

NOTE: In remodeling, bathroom must be at least 5′9″ wide.

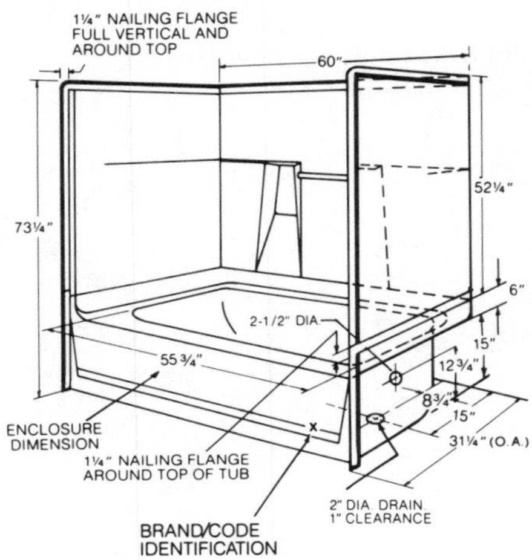
1¼″ NAILING FLANGE FULL VERTICAL AND AROUND TOP
60″
52¼″
73¼″
6″
2-1/2″ DIA.
15″
55 ¾″
12 ¾″
8¾″
15″
31¼″ (O.A.)
ENCLOSURE DIMENSION
1¼″ NAILING FLANGE AROUND TOP OF TUB
2″ DIA. DRAIN 1″ CLEARANCE
BRAND/CODE IDENTIFICATION

THREE-PIECE TUB/SHOWER

2603-TRIO

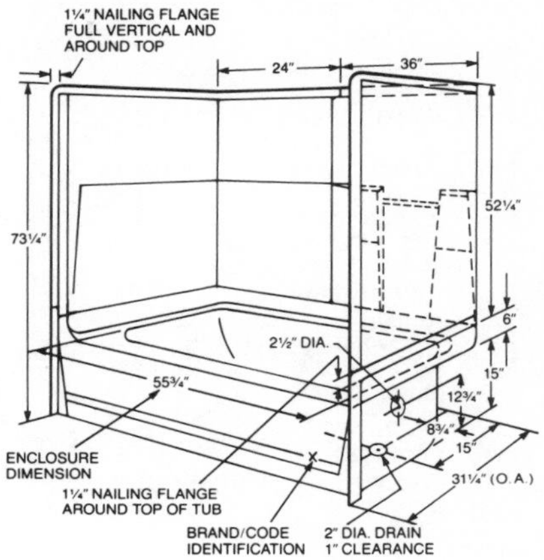
1¼″ NAILING FLANGE FULL VERTICAL AND AROUND TOP
24″
36″
52¼″
73¼″
6″
2½″ DIA.
15″
55¾″
12¾″
8¾″
15″
31¼″ (O.A.)
ENCLOSURE DIMENSION
1¼″ NAILING FLANGE AROUND TOP OF TUB
BRAND/CODE IDENTIFICATION
2″ DIA. DRAIN 1″ CLEARANCE

Before ordering tub enclosures or shower doors, install bath fixture and measure actual opening.

TWO-PIECE SHOWER

1323-2P*

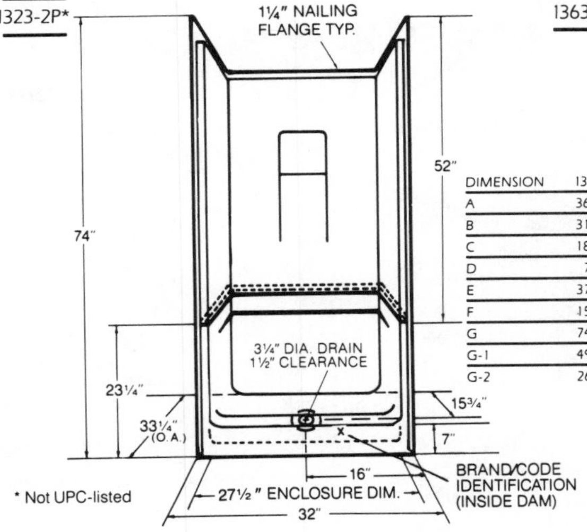
1¼″ NAILING FLANGE TYP.
52″
74″
3¼″ DIA. DRAIN 1½″ CLEARANCE
23¼″
33¼″ (O.A.)
15¾″
7″
16″
27½″ ENCLOSURE DIM.
32″
BRAND/CODE IDENTIFICATION (INSIDE DAM)

* Not UPC-listed

THREE-PIECE (TRIO) SHOWERS

1363-TRIO, 1483-TRIO

DIMENSION	1363-TRIO	1483-TRIO
A	36″	48″
B	31½″	43½″
C	18″	24″
D	7″	7″
E	37¼″	35¼″
F	15¾″	15¾″
G	74″	74″
G-1	49″	52″
G-2	26¼″	23¼″

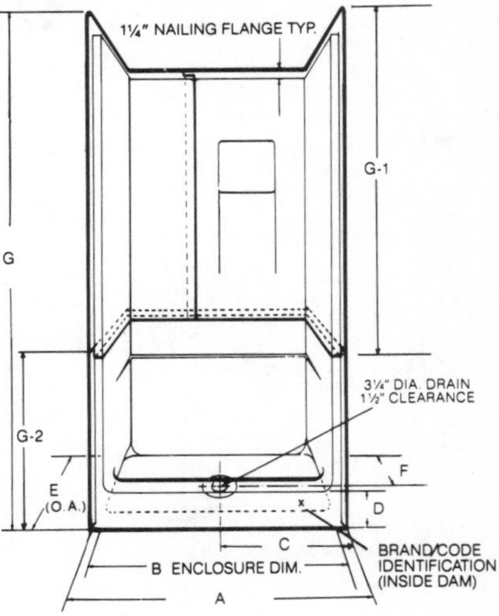
1¼″ NAILING FLANGE TYP.
G-1
G
3¼″ DIA. DRAIN 1½″ CLEARANCE
G-2
F
E (O.A.)
D
C
B ENCLOSURE DIM.
A
BRAND/CODE IDENTIFICATION (INSIDE DAM)

Dimension tolerance: +0″, −⅜″

Fig. 5-19. Typical two- and three-piece shower stalls and tub/shower combinations (Courtesy of Philips Industries, Inc.).

BATHTUB WALLS

Wood or Metal Studs

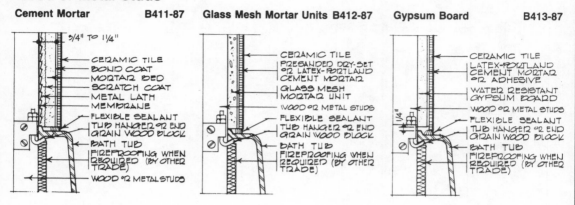

Cement Mortar   B411-87

- 3/4" TO 1 1/4"
- CERAMIC TILE
- BOND COAT
- MORTAR BED
- SCRATCH COAT
- METAL LATH
- MEMBRANE
- FLEXIBLE SEALANT
- TUB HANGER OR END GRAIN WOOD BLOCK
- BATH TUB
- FIREPROOFING WHEN REQUIRED (BY OTHER TRADE)
- WOOD OR METAL STUDS

Glass Mesh Mortar Units B412-87

- CERAMIC TILE
- PRESANDED DRY-SET OR LATEX-PORTLAND CEMENT MORTAR
- GLASS MESH MORTAR UNIT
- WOOD OR METAL STUDS
- FLEXIBLE SEALANT
- TUB HANGER OR END GRAIN WOOD BLOCK
- BATH TUB
- FIREPROOFING WHEN REQUIRED (BY OTHER TRADE)

Gypsum Board   B413-87

- CERAMIC TILE
- LATEX-PORTLAND CEMENT MORTAR OR ADHESIVE
- WATER RESISTANT GYPSUM BOARD
- WOOD OR METAL STUDS
- 1/4"
- FLEXIBLE SEALANT
- TUB HANGER OR END GRAIN WOOD BLOCK
- BATH TUB
- FIREPROOFING WHEN REQUIRED (BY OTHER TRADE)

SHOWER RECEPTORS, WALLS
Wood or Metal Studs

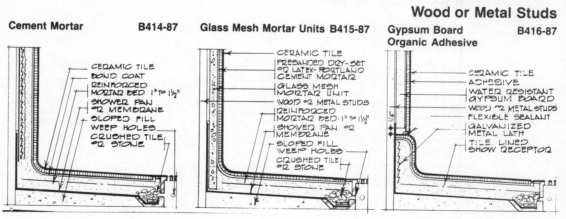

Cement Mortar   B414-87

- CERAMIC TILE
- BOND COAT
- REINFORCED MORTAR BED 1" TO 1/2"
- SHOWER PAN OR MEMBRANE
- SLOPED FILL
- WEEP HOLES
- CRUSHED TILE OR STONE

Glass Mesh Mortar Units B415-87

- CERAMIC TILE
- PRESANDED DRY-SET OR LATEX-PORTLAND CEMENT MORTAR
- GLASS MESH MORTAR UNIT
- WOOD OR METAL STUDS
- REINFORCED MORTAR BED·1" TO 1/2"
- SHOWER PAN OR MEMBRANE
- SLOPED FILL
- WEEP HOLES
- CRUSHED TILE OR STONE

Gypsum Board   B416-87
Organic Adhesive

- CERAMIC TILE
- ADHESIVE
- WATER RESISTANT GYPSUM BOARD
- WOOD OR METAL STUDS
- 1/4"
- FLEXIBLE SEALANT
- GALVANIZED METAL LATH
- TILE LINED SHOW RECEPTOR

Fig. 5-20. Construction details for the installation of ceramic tile surrounds used with a bathtub (top) and a shower pan (bottom) (Courtesy of the Tile Council of America).

Fig. 5-21. A high-quality, cast iron oval sink, shown here with a single-handle faucet (Courtesy of Kohler Co.).

Fig. 5-22. A 9-×-15-inch oval sink with a counter-mounted faucet (Courtesy of Kohler Co.).

Fig. 5-23. A 20-×-16-inch hexagonal sink. The counter-mounted, spread-set faucet allows placement of the handles wherever desired (Courtesy of Kohler Co.).

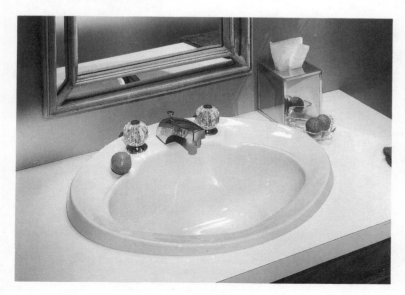

Fig. 5-24. A typical self-rimming sink mounted in a laminate countertop (Courtesy of Universal-Rundle Corporation).

Fig. 5-25. An elegant wall-mounted cultured marble sink and counter, with brass legs for front support (Courtesy of Kohler Co.).

GALLERIA PEDESTAL LAVATORY

0180.054
POP-UP DRAIN

VITREOUS CHINA
SHOWN WITH 2248. SER. FTG.,
3/8 FLEX SUPP., 1-1/4 O.D. "P" TRAP

PEDESTAL ANCHOR SCREW HOLE (3/8 DIA.)
ANCHORING SCREW NOT FURNISHED

FINISHED WALL

2-1/2

7-3/4

19-5/8

8

OUTLINE OF
PEDESTAL

25-3/4

30-1/2

*11-1/4

8-1/4

3/4 DIA. HOLES FOR
ANCHOR SCREWS

7

31-1/2

8

3/8 S.P.S. SUPPLIES

1-1/4 O.D. WASTE

20-1/4

1-1/4 O.D. TAILPIECE

17-1/2

FINISHED FLOOR

▼DIMENSIONS SHOWN FOR LOCATION OF SUPPLIES AND "P" TRAP ARE
SUGGESTED.

*SEE INSTALLATION INSTRUCTIONS SUPPLIED WITH LAVATORY. DIMENSIONS
SUITABLE FOR REINFORCEMENT ONLY, ACTUAL DIMENSIONS MUST BE TAKEN
FROM FIXTURE.

PLUMBER NOTE — Provide suitable reinforcement for all wall supports.

NOTE: FITTINGS NOT INCLUDED WITH FIXTURE AND MUST BE ORDERED SEPARATELY.

IMPORTANT   Dimensions of fixtures are nominal and may vary within the range of
tolerances established by ANSI Standards A112.19.2.

These measurements are subject to change or cancellation.
No responsibility is assumed for use of superseded of voided leaflets.

AMERICAN STANDARD

L263

23

JAN. 1985

Fig. 5-26. A sleek, modern pedestal sink design (Courtesy of American Standard).

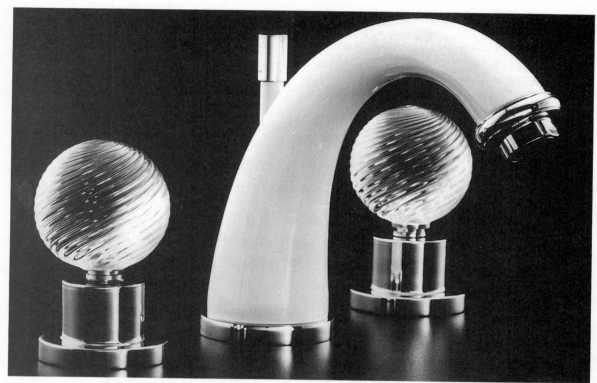

Fig. 5-27. A contemporary three-piece, spread-set bathroom faucet with pop-up (Courtesy of Kohler Co.).

Fig. 5-28. A two-handle faucet designed for mounting on the sink (Courtesy of Stanadyne Moen Group).

also have chrome legs for additional support. Wall-hung sinks are the least expensive of the various sink types and require the least amount of space. Because all the plumbing is exposed underneath, they are usually the least attractive.

Pedestal

Another more attractive alternative if you are not using a vanity is the pedestal sink. Sinks of this type were very popular in years past, and models are available in both old-fashioned and sleek contemporary designs (Fig. 5-26). The pedestal offers good support and easy installation, and hides the pipes from the front. The biggest drawbacks to a pedestal sink are the loss of storage space underneath it and the relatively high cost.

Fig. 5-29. This bathtub features a faucet and filler spout that uses ¾-inch pipe (top) for faster tub filling, and a hand-held, single-handle personal shower nozzle (bottom) (Courtesy of Interbath).

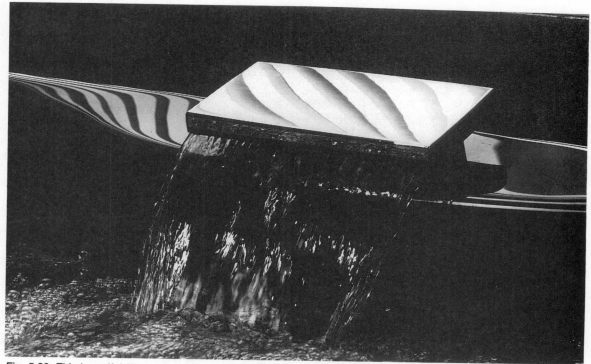

Fig. 5-30. This beautiful filler spout creates a waterfall as it fills the bathtub (Courtesy of Jacuzzi Whirlpool Bath).

FAUCETS AND SHOWER SETS

Shopping for faucets can be even more bewildering than shopping for fixtures. You will have a choice between single-handle and two-handle controls, wall- and deck-mounted sets, center-set and spread-set designs, ½-inch and ¾-inch supplies, standard and water-saving, and a staggering variety of styles and finishes. (See Figs. 5-27 through 5-33.)

Faucets range in price from under $20.00 to hundreds or even thousands of dollars. They are one item where price is not always a reliable indicator of quality. Much of what you are paying for with a faucet is the finish, which can range from thin, cheap chrome plating to finishes of real gold. Quite often, you'll find the underlying faucet mechanisms are basically the same.

Initially, you will want to look for a faucet from a reputable manufacturer. The workings should be solid brass for corrosion resistance and long life, and should operate smoothly and seat well. From there you are pretty much on your own, and your final choice will be dictated by the style and finish that best fits your decor, and by how well that style and finish fits your budget.

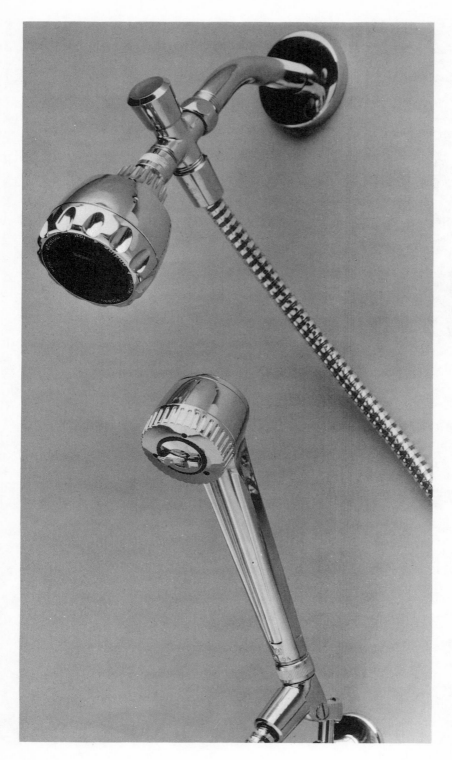

Fig. 5-31. This shower head arrangement allows you to choose between a conventional shower head (top) and a hand-held sprayer (bottom) (Courtesy of Interbath).

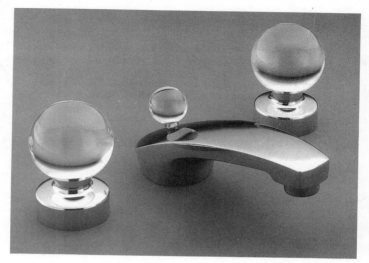

Fig. 5-32. Another beautifully-designed contemporary bathtub filler set, intended for platform mounting next to a sunken bathtub (Courtesy of Stanadyne Moen Group).

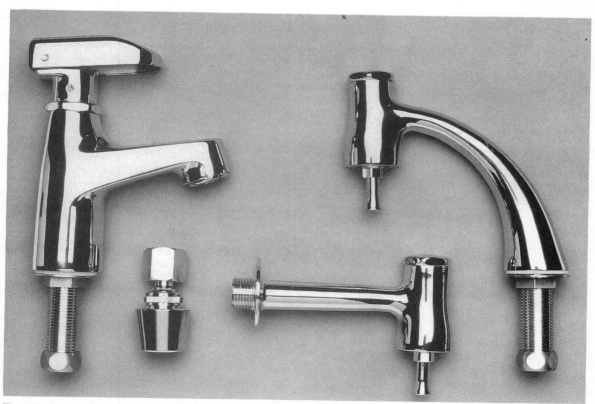

Fig. 5-33. A sample of some of the self-closing faucets and low-flow shower heads now on the market (Courtesy of Microphor).

Chapter 6

Whirlpools, Saunas, and Steam Baths

A REALLY EXCITING CONCEPT OF TODAY'S BATH-room is their change in focus. Once a simple, purely functional area where a minimum of time was spent, the modern bathroom is a haven for relaxation, an attractive oasis for a quiet time alone or with a special friend, to revive the senses and rejuvenate the spirit. Nowhere is this new awareness of the bathroom's possibilities seen more clearly than in the increasing popularity of saunas, steam rooms, and whirlpool spas and bathtubs.

Once large, commercial "health spa" equipment only, whirlpools, saunas, and steam equipment have been scaled down and dressed up in recent years, and have found a large and enthusiastic new market for use in the home. A surprising variety of equipment is available for home use, meeting the needs of the individual or the whole family, large or small. Decorator colors and styles, easier installation, reduced energy consumption, simplified do-it-yourself kits, and lower prices have combined to make this type of equipment a very attractive and affordable addition to your new bathroom.

While most whirlpools, saunas, and steam baths are relatively easy to add to your bathroom remodeling project, their addition requires thorough planning. With the exception of some whirlpool tubs, which will fit in the space formerly occupied by a con-

ventional bathtub, much of this equipment is fairly large. Even the placement of a small 4- × -4-foot sauna takes some careful planning—after all, that additional 16 square feet of floor space has to come from somewhere.

In addition to space considerations, most of the equipment will require special electrical lines or plumbing work. Although these requirements are usually not extensive or complicated, you do need to plan for them in advance. If a whirlpool, sauna, or steam bath will be part of your new bathroom—and they're certainly worth considering—make your decisions and choices early. This early decision will give you the opportunity to plan for space and utility requirements; for ordering and shipping time, which can often be several weeks; and for whatever impact the purchase is going to have on your budget.

HEALTH CONSIDERATIONS

For centuries people all over the world have used saunas and steam baths, and there are thousands of people who use them regularly and extol their virtues. Whirlpool baths are newcomers by comparison; however, many people have used them for decades with great results.

A number of very positive health benefits are

associated with whirlpools, saunas, and steam baths. Some of these benefits are real, backed up by scientific research and medical evidence; others might be just a product of the user's relaxed state of mind. At the very least, having access to this type equipment in the privacy and convenience of your own home can offer relaxation, stress reduction, and just plain fun.

Some risks are involved, though, and you should not take them lightly. Sauna manufacturers warn against use by people suffering from heart disease or high blood pressure, particularly the elderly; warnings commonly are extended to pregnant women also. The same cautions are true for whirlpools and steam baths, where prolonged exposure to high temperatures might aggravate certain existing medical problems.

Be sure to carefully read any literature that accompanies your new whirlpool, sauna, or steam bath. Pay particular attention to the health warnings. If you have any questions or concerns, consult with your physician first. In any case, no matter what the state of your health, never use whirlpools, saunas, and steam baths while under the influence of alcohol or any type of drugs or medication—the combination can be deadly!

WHIRLPOOLS

By far the most common ''luxury'' addition to today's bathroom is the whirlpool bathtub (Fig. 6-1).

Fig. 6-1. An acrylic whirlpool bathtub with waterfall filler spout, set in a raised platform (Courtesy of Jacuzzi Whirlpool Bath).

Manufacturers have introduced whirlpool tubs in dozens of shapes, sizes, styles, and colors. Like the microwave oven, whirlpools have come to be an accepted, almost essential, part of the master bathroom suite in upscale new homes. This acceptance in new construction has affected remodeling also, and many designers routinely are including a whirlpool tub in their plans when redesigning an existing room.

Prior to the 1950s, whirlpool technology was big, bulky, expensive, and used almost exclusively by hospital therapy centers for treating certain illnesses and injuries. Then, in 1956, the Jacuzzi Whirlpool Bath Company introduced the first whirlpool pump. The pump was portable and freestanding, designed to be hung over the side of an existing bathtub. Hydrotherapy now had made it into the home for the first time, but it was still something used primarily by professional athletes, dancers, and people undergoing continuing therapy at the recommendation of their doctor.

Then, in 1968, the first self-contained whirlpool bathtub was introduced for the home market. People who had never heard of whirlpools had the opportunity to experience their relaxing benefits, and the market has grown ever since. As the demand has increased and more companies have introduced whirlpool tubs into their lines of bathroom fixtures, the selection has increased and the prices have dropped.

The concept of the whirlpool bath is simple. A small pump draws bath water from inside the tub through an intake line, then forces it out through other lines to "jets" located at strategic spots within the tub. Air, brought in through separate intakes, is mixed with the water to produce the familiar bubbling effect. It is this combination of warmth and moving, aerated water that makes the whirlpool bath so effective in soothing sore muscles.

Whirlpool Bathtubs

The first whirlpool tubs were designed to fit in the same space formerly occupied by a "standard" rectangular bathtub—5 × 2½ feet. Because of the space limitations commonly associated with remodel-ing, this size remains the most common whirlpool tub size today.

If you like to stretch out and if you have the extra room with which to work, you might want to consider an oversized one-person tub, or even a two-person tub. (See Fig. 6-2.) Some typical sizes for these larger tubs include 5-foot units that are 3, 3½, or 4 feet wide, and 6-foot units in the same range of widths.

Most whirlpool tubs are designed to be installed in a raised platform or in an opening in the floor, and as such are open on all four sides. Some models are available with a factory-installed panel on one side for conventional installation, and many manufacturers also offer an optional side panel that can be attached to the tub onsite during installation.

Whirlpool bathtubs are prepared fully at the factory (Fig. 6-3), and are almost as easy to install as a conventional bathtub. All the supply and return lines are in place, as are the jets and the pump, and the entire system has been tested to ensure proper, no-leak operation. After you have set the tub in place and secured it, all you need to do is bring an electrical circuit to the pump motor, and provide an access opening in front of the pump to facilitate future servicing. A conventional bathtub faucet supplies water to the tub and it uses a standard drain and trap setup.

Whirlpool Spas

If you have a large family or if you entertain a lot and would like to share the pleasures of a whirlpool with your friends, you might want to consider a whirlpool spa. Spas are considerably larger than whirlpool tubs, with the capacity to seat four or six people comfortably.

The basic principle of the whirlpool spa is the same as the whirlpool tub: heated, aerated water is circulated by a pump and injected under pressure through jets within the spa enclosure. There are two very big differences, however. Because of the volume of water a spa holds (200 to 400 gallons, as opposed to around 50 to 75 gallons for a bathtub), spas are not filled and drained with each use. Like a swim-

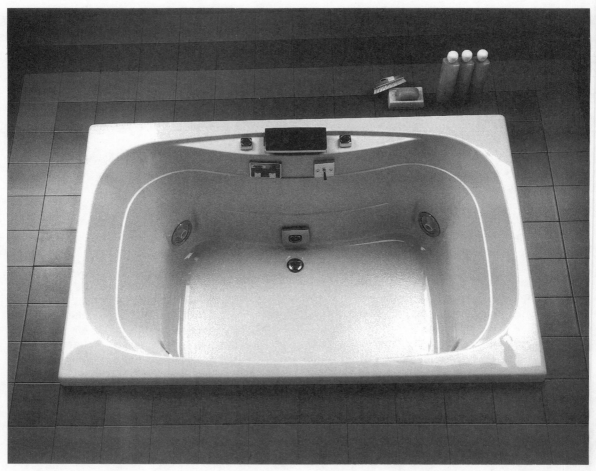

Fig. 6-2. A high-quality, two-person whirlpool bathtub, shown here sunken into the ceramic tile floor. The filler spout and handles are at the top of the tub and just below those are the whirlpool controls (left) and the handle (right) for closing the drain (bottom of tub). The square fitting at the bottom of the side wall is the return inlet for drawing water back into the pump, and there is an adjustable jet in each of the four corners (Courtesy of Jacuzzi Whirlpool Bath).

ming pool, after you have filled the spa, the water remains in it, being filtered and chemically treated as necessary to maintain a safe and pleasant level of cleanliness. The other difference is that the spa requires its own heater to achieve and maintain the desired water temperature.

Spas can be purchased in with or without an enclosure. Spas sold without an enclosure (Fig. 6-4), are treated similar to an in-ground swimming pool. Typically, you excavate a hole in the ground, then partially fill it with sand. You then set the spa in the hole so that the sand surrounds and supports the underside of it, then you cover the area around it with a patio or deck. You should run lines from the spa to a remote location that houses the filter and heater.

Portable Spas

A relative newcomer on the scene is the self-contained portable spa, (Fig. 6-5). Growing rapidly in popularity, the portable spa has several advantages over the in-ground spa. Portable spas come

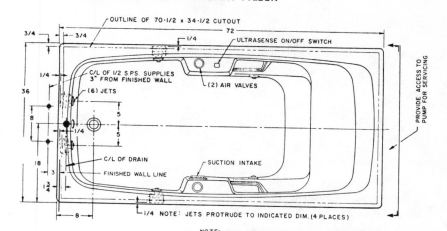
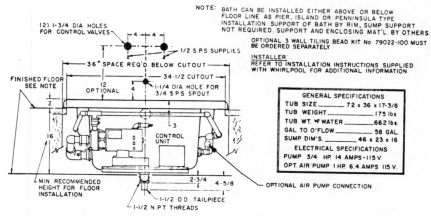

Fig. 6-3. An example of how the motor, motor controls, and plumbing are arranged and installed on a complete, factory-plumbed whirlpool bathtub. A tub such as this one is ready to be set into a platform or into the floor, requiring only drain and electrical connections (Courtesy of American Standard).

Fig. 6-4. An octagonal whirlpool spa mounted into an outdoor wooden deck. A spa such as this one can comfortably accommodate up to six adults (Courtesy of Jacuzzi Whirlpool Bath).

Fig. 6-5. One of the growing number of portable, self-contained whirlpool spas. This spa features two built-in skimmers, four directionally-adjustable jets, full foam insulation, and a rigid thermal spa cover (Courtesy of Jacuzzi Whirlpool Bath).

completely wrapped within a wooden enclosure, usually redwood, cedar, or other moisture-resistant wood. Within the enclosure is all the plumbing, the filtration system, and an electric heater. (Gas heaters are available from some manufacturers as an option.) The spa itself is insulated well with a sprayed-on foam insulation coating, and a single small door in the side of the enclosure gives access to all the electrical and mechanical equipment.

The initial cost of a portable spa is higher because of the enclosure, but there are no installation costs at the job site. The spa is ready for immediate use, requiring only one electrical connection. Best of all, if you move to another house or remodel the one you are in, you can move the spa easily to a new location.

The area required for a whirlpool spa is obviously greater than the area required for a bathtub, ranging from about 5 × 5 feet to around 7 × 7 feet. If you are planning a large exercise area adjacent to the bathroom, it might be the ideal location for a spa, either portable or built-in. Other possibilities include an inside or outside garden area off the bathroom, an open patio, or a small, glass-enclosed sunroom. Many designers are creating dedicated leisure/entertainment/exercise areas with a multiperson spa as the focal point.

SELECTING A WHIRLPOOL BATHTUB OR SPA

Increasing competition among manufacturers and dealers is good and bad. The selection of sizes, colors, styles, and options available today is greater, and prices have come down. However, a little more shopping will be required on your part to ensure that you are getting the best quality and the right features for your money. Here are some tips when shopping for a whirlpool bathtub or spa:

☐ Visit a showroom that offers a selection of manufacturers, sizes, and prices so you can effectively and conveniently examine a cross section of what is on the market.

☐ Be sure any tub or spa you buy has been tested and approved by Underwriter's Laboratories (UL) or the International Association of Plumb-

ing and Mechanical Officials (IAPMO) to ensure your safety. Certification will be displayed prominently on the unit and in the manufacturer's literature. It's best to stay away from any unit that has not been tested and approved.

☐ Check the location and adjustment of the jets to be certain they are comfortable and adequate for your needs. Try to see the tub or spa you are interested in when it is filled and in operation, and check the massage action of the jets.

☐ Check the controls for placement, convenience, and safety.

☐ Talk to the dealer about installation requirements. If this will be a do-it-yourself installation, look for a unit that is within your capabilities.

☐ Compare the filtration systems, heaters, and maintenance requirements of each unit. Ask for and compare the estimated energy usage of each unit also. Look for a spa that is energy efficient and easy to maintain.

☐ When purchasing a spa, be sure you get an insulated cover for it, even if it costs extra. The cover will help maintain the temperature of the water in the spa, and prevent a child or pet from accidentally falling into it. Some types can be locked to prevent unauthorized entry. Look for a strong, rigid, well-insulated cover; with the flexible covers that float on the surface, a child or pet that steps on the cover can become easily entangled in it and drown.

☐ Talk to the dealer about the warranties and know exactly what they cover. Inquire about the reputation of the manufacturer, and the availability of after-installation servicing.

☐ Talk to a few of the dealer's past customers to see if they are satisfied with the product and the service, if possible.

When installing the whirlpool, consider these safety and convenience tips also:

☐ With a multiperson spa, carefully consider who will be using it and where the most convenient location will be. Look at traffic patterns, access to the house or to separate changing facilities for guests, and privacy and weather protection if the spa is to be outside.

☐ Consider designing a room around other activities you would enjoy along with your whirlpool, such as reading, television, music, or exercise. However, be certain the electrical devices are grounded and at least 5 feet away from the whirlpool. Under no circumstances should you be able to reach the controls of any electrical device from within the tub or spa.

☐ Limit your initial use of the whirlpool to 10 to 15 minutes, and cool down after exercising before entering the water.

☐ Limit the water temperature to a maximum of about 105°F.

Custom Whirlpools

If your new bathroom includes a custom-built bathtub (see Chapter 5), it does not mean that you cannot have a whirlpool. Manufacturers can build the pump and all of the necessary plumbing into any custom tub design. (See Fig. 6-6.)

After the basic framework of the tub is completed, you need to install an intake screen near the foot of the tub. In this installation you should use rigid or flexible plastic pipe to connect the intake fitting to the intake side of the pump. You can place the jets as you desire, and use additional pipe to connect the jets to the outlet side of the pump. You should install the jets within the framework enclosing the tub before you waterproof the tub. When you follow this procedure, you can seal the jets into place to prevent leakage. Finally, place the pump in a convenient location, such as under the backrest of the tub, and provide an access door to it for future servicing.

When planning a custom whirlpool, discuss your design and your needs with a reputable spa dealer. He can provide you with the proper jets and pump for your installation, and can direct you on how and where to place them within the tub for the best results.

SAUNAS

The exact origins of the sauna are unclear, but it has been a well-recorded part of the culture of many civilizations for centuries. Saunas are most associated with the Finns; however, Russians, Islams, Japanese, Mexicans, American Indians, and even the Eskimos, have enjoyed saunas in some form. More recently, with the increased awareness of physical fitness and good health and the resultant growth of public gyms and health spas, people from all walks of life have discovered and enjoyed the sauna.

A *sauna* is essentially a large, wooden room with a single door, benches, and a heater. Somewhat stark in appearance at first glance, they are nonetheless quite comfortable and attractive in their own right, with wide seating and beautiful interiors of natural wood. (See Fig. 6-7.) Redwood, hemlock, cedar, spruce, aspen, and pine are common sauna woods because they have the ability to withstand moisture and maintain a relatively cool surface temperature.

The principle of the modern sauna is very simple: an electric heater warms a layer of rocks, which in turn absorb and hold the heat, releasing it slowly to the room. The dry heat is said to relax muscles, open the pores and cleanse the skin, and induce a calm state of mind. A traditional wooden bucket and dipper sprinkles over the rocks as desired to maintain a comfortable level of humidity and prevent the air from becoming too dry. Certain aromatic leaves and oils, particularly eucalyptus, often are placed in the sauna room to add their fragrance and beneficial effects to the air.

Tradition has it that, after using the sauna, the Scandinavians would run outside and jump in the snow to cool down. While you might not want to go to that extreme, there are benefits to cooling down with a cold shower afterward. Cold water on warm skin is thought to have the effect of stimulating and arousing both respiration and circulation.

Home Saunas

The introduction of scaled-down saunas for residential use has increased their popularity tremendously. People who were first introduced to the sauna at their health club have discovered that they can have the same soothing, relaxing benefits in their own home. A basement, attic, or walk-in closet can easily be adapted to fit a sauna, but their installation

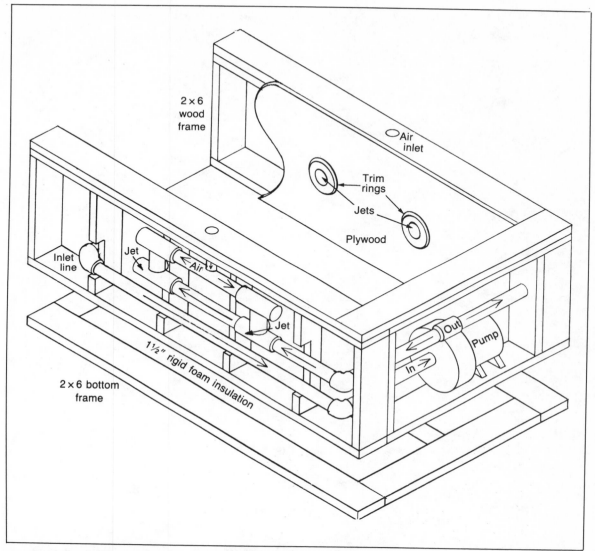

Fig. 6-6. An example of the construction details for a site-built, custom whirlpool bathtub. The tub is built from a 2- × -6 wood frame covered with ¾-inch exterior plywood, and sits on a 2- × -6 frame and 1½-inch rigid foam insulation for heat retention. After the tub frame and plumbing are in place, the walls are insulated and the outside is covered with plywood. The interior of the tub is then hot-tarred, and the entire unit is finished with ceramic tile.

in the bathroom is a natural. (See Fig. 6-8.) The close proximity of changing and showering facilities make a bathroom sauna ideal.

Saunas for the home come in two basic forms: modular packages (Fig. 6-9) and precut kits. Both forms contain everything you need to complete and install the sauna, including all interior lumber and trim, a door with tempered glass window and hardware, a properly sized heater for the dimensions of the sauna you have purchased, all necessary controls, and accessories such as a bucket and dipper, interior light, and head and backrests. The modular units also include exterior lumber and trim, and insulation.

Fig. 6-7. The inviting, beautifully-appointed interior of a home sauna. There is an outward-opening wood door with glass insert (left); a thermometer for measuring inside air temperature (top center); multi-level seating with back rests; nonslip duck boards on the floor; and a protective guard rail around the heater (lower left). The bucket and ladle are for spooning water over the hot rocks in the heater (Courtesy of Amerec).

Available sizes vary among manufacturers (Fig. 6-10), but in general you will find units ranging in size from as small as 3 × 4 feet up to 10 × 12 feet or larger. Most of the larger manufacturers also will custom-make a sauna, in kit or modular form, to almost any dimensions you specify.

Shop around and choose carefully when purchasing a sauna. You want to select a unit that is large enough to suit your current and projected future needs, but you do not want to buy one that is too large. Large units eat up more space, are more expensive initially, require larger and more expensive electrical wiring, and cost more to heat. The amount of space you have available obviously will be a major factor in selecting the size of the sauna, as will the number of people who will be using it at any one time. Most manufacturers recommend about 2 feet of upper bench space for each person the sauna will accommodate.

As with other major purchases, you must con-

Fig. 6-8. A home sauna, built from a kit, which has been integrated into a remodeled bathroom. A bathroom sauna is an ideal arrangement for convenience and privacy. Saunas such as this one require only one electrical connection and no plumbing (Courtesy of Helo Sauna and Fitness).

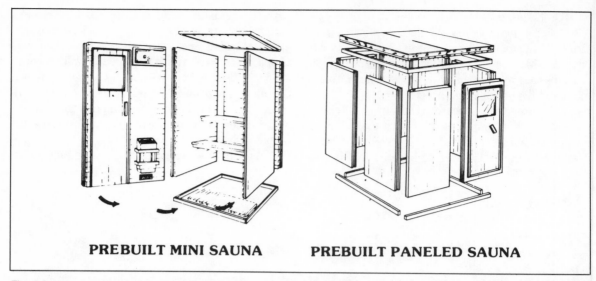

PREBUILT MINI SAUNA   **PREBUILT PANELED SAUNA**

Fig. 6-9. An example of prebuilt, modular sauna packages for home installation (Courtesy of Helo Sauna and Fitness).

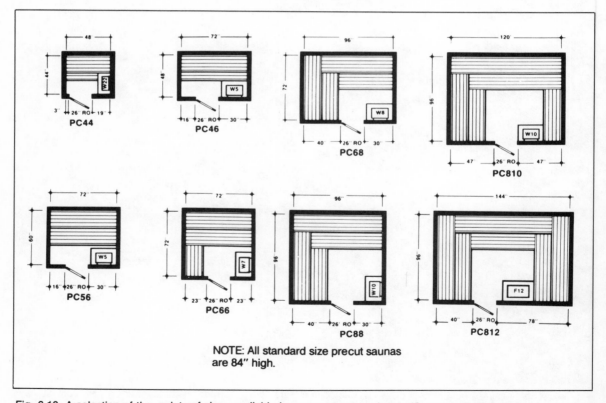

NOTE: All standard size precut saunas are 84" high.

Fig. 6-10. A selection of the variety of sizes available in precut sauna packages (Courtesy of Amerec).

sider several other things when selecting a sauna. Look for a reputable dealer with a reputable product. Check the warranties and service available from the dealer, including the availability of technical and installation advice should you need it. Consider your budget and your ability to assemble the kit or modular package. Also, always look for a UL-tested and rated product to ensure your safety.

Modular Sauna Packages

Modular packages are designed primarily to allow you to construct a freestanding sauna. (See Figs. 6-11 & 6-12.) These packages have more of the work already done at the factory, so they require less work to assemble and install than the kits. For this reason, modular packages are somewhat more expensive.

The walls and ceiling are shipped in preassembled and preinsulated modular sections, with installation instructions. Assembly of the sections is simple and is done on-site, usually in just a few hours. Because these are freestanding rooms, the wall sections have an exterior covering, as well as an interior one, which also adds to the cost.

Most of the electrical wiring already has been done; the majority of modular sauna packages require only the installation of the light and heater, and connection to an outside electrical supply source. A

Fig. 6-11. A two-person, modular sauna which operates on 110-volt power and can be constructed in about an hour (Courtesy of Helo Sauna and Fitness).

separate electrical circuit for the sauna is required, sized to the particular heater you are using. Some models are 110 volt, and require as little as a 15-amp circuit. Larger units require 220 volts with circuit capacities of as much as 65 amps. Before ordering a sauna, be sure to check with a qualified electrician to see if your electrical service panel has the necessary capacity.

Precut Sauna Kits

If you are in the process of building or remodeling your bathroom, a good alternative to the modular package is the sauna kit. Sauna kits are designed to finish off an already prepared room or alcove. You frame in the area to the manufacturer's rough opening specifications, wire and drywall it, then use the materials in the kit to finish it off. Because there's less factory labor involved and there's no exterior to worry about, the kits are less expensive than the modular packages. In addition, you get a more finished, "built-in" look.

The kit comes with all the necessary lumber already cut. All you do is install it in the room, usually in a matter of just a few hours. Most manufacturers ship the kits with the benches preassembled for quick installation.

If you intend to incorporate a built-in sauna using one of the precut kits, consult with a dealer while you are still in the early planning stages. You will need the manufacturer's dimensions so you can frame the room to fit one of the standard kits. If your space will not fit one of the kits, however, many manufacturers will design a custom kit to suit your area.

General Sauna Precautions

You can decorate the outside of a sauna any way you wish; however, do not use surface treatments of any kind on the interior! Stains and paints can make inside surfaces slippery, and many emit toxic fumes when heated.

The door of the sauna must always open out.

Fig. 6-12. A freestanding, 5-×-7-foot sauna with seating for the entire family (Courtesy of Helo Sauna and Fitness).

This requirement is a safety precaution in case someone inside becomes dizzy or disoriented. In addition, the inside door handle should be made of wood, and no locking devices of any kind, interior or exterior, should be used. If you want to prevent a child from using a sauna unsupervised, shut off the circuit breaker to it instead of locking or securing the door another way.

As mentioned previously, if you are elderly, pregnant, or suffer from heart disease or high blood pressure, consult with your physician before using a sauna. Elderly people should also cool down gradually, avoiding the shock of a cold shower afterward.

Never use a sauna when you are under the influence of alcohol or drugs.

STEAM BATHS

Like the sauna, the origins of the steam bath are lost in history. A variety of cultures have enjoyed them over the centuries, and in some countries, the steam bath is still the traditional way to close a business deal or end a busy day.

The benefits of a steam bath are, in many ways, similar to those of the sauna. Heat, in this case moist instead of dry, penetrates and loosens tight muscles. The steam also opens skin pores and offers a deep-cleaning action that many find beneficial. However, also like the sauna, probably the greatest virtue of the steam bath is relaxation and an overall feeling of well being.

Some experts maintain that there is an ''art'' to taking a steam bath. They suggest you begin with a shower, then enter the steam bath. Settle yourself comfortably, and enjoy the steam. Get out of the steam bath and cool down with a shower, then go back to the steam. Finally, finish by soaping and rinsing in a cool shower.

Dedicated Steam Rooms

If you have enjoyed a steam bath in the past, it was probably at a gym in a steam room that was specifically designed for this purpose. As with the trend in scaling down other gymnasium equipment for residential use, steam rooms of this type are available now for use in the home.

Most rooms of this type are self-contained, and are shipped from the factory completely ready for use. All that is required is a place to set the unit, a drain connection (as the steam cools and condenses, it turns back into water and needs someplace to go), and water and electrical connections for the steamer. You can leave the room freestanding, or build it into the room (Fig. 6-13), so that only the door is visible from the outside.

Many of these dedicated steam rooms now feature essentially seamless fiberglass or acrylic interiors for easy maintenance, are well lit, and are available in several colors. One manufacturer even offers one with a transparent acrylic dome for a ceiling to maximize natural light inside the room.

Steam Generators

If you think you might like an occasional steam bath but are reluctant to invest in a complete steam room, a steam generator might be the perfect solution. Used in conjunction with your existing shower or bathtub, it offers the enjoyment of steam with a minimum of space and expense.

The remote steam generator is located in any convenient spot within about 20 feet of the bath area. (See Fig. 6-14.) They are relatively small, about 16 × 20 × 5 inches, and can be placed in a vanity cabinet, under the floor, or in the attic. Only three connections are necessary: a water line to supply the steamer with water, a steam line to carry the steam from the steamer to the bath enclosure, and an electrical line to power the steamer. A special steam head, installed in the bath enclosure, distributes the steam, and thermostatic controls outside the enclosure regulate the temperature. When you are done with the steam bath, simply shut the steamer and turn on the cold water in the shower. The steam will condense quickly back to water and run out through the shower's drain.

If you intend to convert your tub or shower for use with a steamer, you will need to equip the enclosure with sliding doors, rather than a shower curtain. Use tall doors that reach the ceiling of the enclosure or an extra panel above the doors in order to trap the steam within the enclosure.

Fig. 6-13. An attractive modern steamroom that has been built into a bathroom (Courtesy of Amerec).

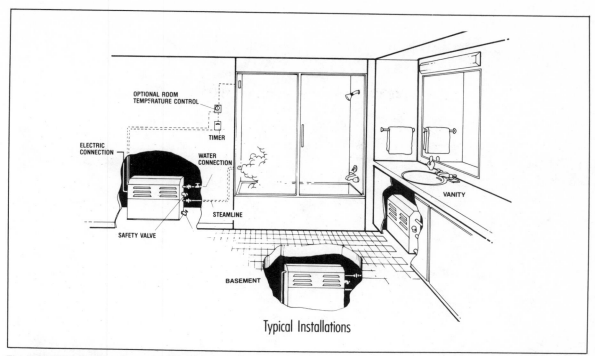

Typical Installations

Fig. 6-14. Some of the many possible locations for a steam generator that is used in conjunction with an existing shower or tub/shower combination (Courtesy of Lattner Boiler).

THE ENVIRONMENT MASTERBATH AND ENVIRONMENT HABITAT

No discussion of whirlpools, saunas, and steam baths would be complete without mentioning the ultimate combination of all three, and more—the Environment Masterbath and the Environment Habitat, manufactured by the Kohler Company.

The Masterbath (Fig. 6-15), is an attractive all-in-one, self-contained unit that is probably the single most unashamedly luxurious bathroom fixture on the market today. Electronic controls offer a variety of cycles that recreate some of nature's most soothing climactic conditions. As Kohler describes it, the cycles include "sauna, to open your pores, stimulate and relax you; steam to totally envelope you; wind to dry and caress you; sun lamps for year-round deep-down warmth; and rain, a gentle spring shower to warm and refresh tired muscles." Each environmental condition can be selected individually, or they can be preprogrammed in any desired se-

quence and for varying amounts of time. Finally, remove the enclosure's padded deck, and beneath is a six-jet, two-person whirlpool bathtub!

Other amenities provided within the Masterbath include gold-plated faucets, showerhead, and trim; a built-in towel cabinet; lighted towel bars; a hand-held showerhead; and simple touch-controls for programming the cycles. The unit is constructed from fiberglass-reinforced acrylic, with a teakwood interior. A less expensive version, the Habitat, has an all-acrylic interior, polished chrome faucets and trim, and a cypress deck.

The Masterbath and the Habitat are not exactly inexpensive. On the other hand, if you are thinking of including an individual whirlpool, sauna, steamroom, and sun lamps, an all-in-one unit might make sense. Also, with dimensions of 91 × 52 × 82 inches (about 33 square feet of floor space), it will probably take up less floor space than a combination of all the individual units.

Fig. 6-15. Kohler's beautifully constructed multi-function Environment Masterbath, shown here integrated into a family bathroom (Courtesy of Kohler Co.).

Chapter 7

Plumbing the Bathroom

A S YOUR PLANS FOR THE NEW BATHROOM COME together and you have purchased and planned for most of the fixtures, it is time to consider the actual construction phases of the project. If your bathroom remodeling will entail any plumbing or electrical work, you will need to decide how much of it you want to do yourself and how much you will need to hire out to contractors.

This chapter will discuss your home's basic plumbing system, along with a discussion of the tools, materials, and procedures involved in working with a typical bathroom remodeling project.

GETTING STARTED

The average bathroom, with all the fixtures grouped within a relatively small area, has considerably more plumbing than any other room in the house. Do not let this plumbing be a deterrent, though. A moderately experienced do-it-yourselfer, equipped with the right tools and a little patience, can tackle most or all of the plumbing procedures encountered in an average bathroom.

Take your time, and familiarize yourself with the plumbing layout as it now exists. Look at the home's overall plumbing system, even if it means a trip under the house or into the attic. While you are at it,

make a "map" of the system, showing where each line originates, where it terminates, and the size and type pipe used. This "map" might seem like extra work, but if you are unfamiliar with plumbing, a thorough understanding of the system and how you will tie into it is essential.

A complete residential plumbing system is actually two separate systems which work together. One is the water supply system, the other is the drain-waste-vent (DWV) system.

THE WATER SYSTEM

The system of water pipes, naturally, supplies hot and cold water to the home's fixtures and faucets. The system originates from the supply source, which might be a municipal water system, a private water supplier, or a private or community well. The water enters the house from the supply source through a single pipe, typically known as the *main*. A valve, located on the main either just before or just after entering the house (Fig. 7-1), is used to shut off the water supply to the entire house.

You will need to be certain that you know the location of this valve and whether it's working properly. Take the time to find and check it before starting any plumbing project. If, after shutting the valve

Fig. 7-1. A main water supply shut-off valve (right), located next to the pressure tank and control cables for a private well.

One line, usually ¾ inch in diameter and taken off the main line fairly near where it enters the house, supplies cold water to the water heater. From the water heater, one or more ¾-inch lines carry hot water to each area, where again the larger lines drop down to the individual ½-inch pipes that supply the fixtures.

At each fixture, you will find small valves called *stops*, which are used to shut off the water supply to a particular faucet or fixture. There will be an individual stop for each line, hot and cold, going to a particular faucet or fixture. If a faucet or fixture needs to be repaired or replaced, the stops allow the water to be shut off directly at the faucet, rather than shutting off the water to the entire house.

Stops should be located directly beneath each sink, and also beneath each toilet (bathtubs and showers typically do not have stops on their lines). Locate and test the operation of each stop in the bathroom, and plan to replace any that do not work correctly.

If you live in a cold climate, you often will find all of the water lines slope slightly to a common low point. A valve at this point allows water in the system to be drained off if the home is to be left vacant for an extended period. If your house is equipped with a system drain of this type, you will want to take care that any new water lines you add are sloped slightly in the proper direction.

THE DRAIN-WASTE-VENT (DWV) SYSTEM

The other main plumbing system in your home is the drain-waste-vent system (Fig. 7-3), commonly abbreviated DWV. The DWV system is actually three smaller systems working in unison, and is usually a little more difficult for the beginning plumber to understand. Take a little time to follow the lines from each of the fixtures in the bathroom you'll be working on—understanding the layout ahead of time and knowing where and how you will tie into it can save you a lot of time and headaches.

Drain lines extend off the bathtub, shower, and bathroom sinks, and are intended to carry liquid waste only. Larger diameter waste lines, also called *soil lines*, extend off the toilets and kitchen sink, and are designed to carry both liquid and solid waste.

entirely, water continues to flow out of each fixture, you have a bad main shutoff valve. Replacing the main shutoff requires the water coming to the house from the source, for example, the city water supply, be shut off. Unless you are experienced with plumbing procedures, replacing a main shutoff should be done by a qualified plumber.

From the main, cold-water lines branch off into separate runs. A larger diameter line, usually ¾ or 1 inch (Fig. 7-2), will run to each area of the house where plumbing exists, the kitchen or a bathroom for example, and will then branch off into individual ½-inch lines to supply each fixture.

Fig. 7-2. One of the home's main cold water supply lines, going to a group of bathroom fixtures on the second floor. Note the plastic clips used to support the pipe above the joist blocking.

Both drain and waste lines empty into the main soil stack, and from there into the building drain. The building drain conveys the waste to a municipal sewer system or private septic tank.

Drain, waste, and soil lines all work by gravity. A slight slope to the pipes, called *fall*, allows the waste to flow down and out of the house. The pipes should fall ¼ inch for each foot of horizontal run; for example, a 10 foot-long waste pipe would be 2½ inches lower where it ties into the soil line than it is at the fixture.

Maintaining the proper fall in the pipes you install is extremely important. If you have too little fall, the waste in the pipes won't flow; too much fall and the liquid waste will flow out faster than the solid waste, creating the possibility of a clogged line.

The third part of the DWV system is the vent pipes. Vents serve a dual purpose in the plumbing system: they provide air to maintain the proper atmospheric pressure in the drain and waste lines, allowing the waste in the system to flow smoothly, and they allow sewer gases to escape to the outside of the home.

You should provide vent pipes for each fixture, and either tie into a single large vent, called the *main vent stack*, or exit through the roof on their own. Vents are set up in one of four ways: (See Fig. 7-4.)

☐ Wet vent: This setup is the easiest and probably the most common vent arrangement, in which you vent the fixture directly through the drain line to the soil pipe;

☐ Back vent: Also called a *loop vent* or *revent*, back vents extend up to connect with another vent at a higher level;

☐ Secondary vent: Also called an individual vent, a secondary vent extends up through the roof by itself, without tying into the main vent stack. Secondary vents are common when a group of fixtures is located a distance away from the home's other plumbing, as in the case of a bathroom that's been added.

☐ Indirect venting: Indirect venting occurs when a drain line dumps into an open drain without any other venting. A typical example of this type venting would be a washing machine drain that emp-

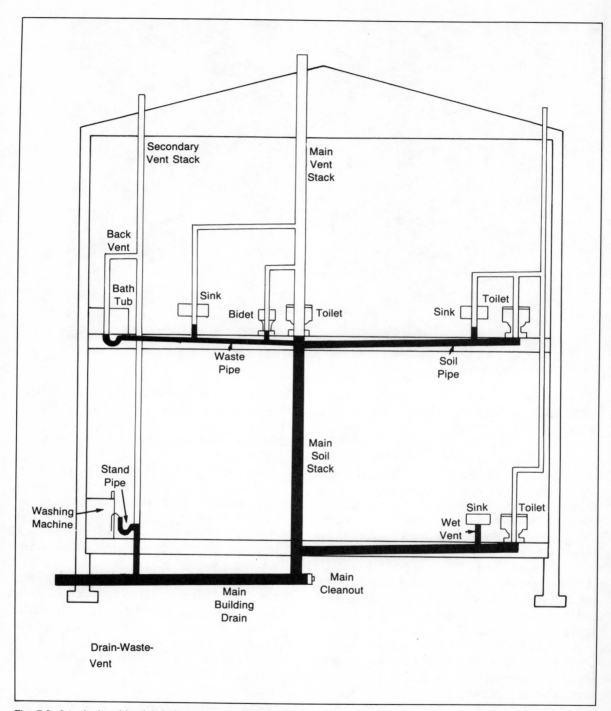

Fig. 7-3. A typical residential drain-waste-vent (DWV) system.

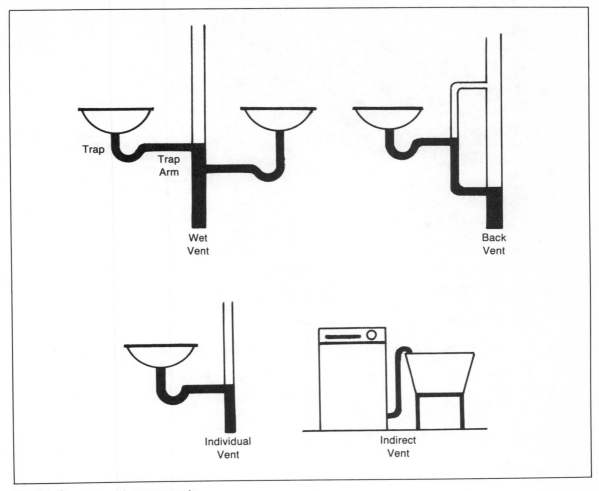

Fig. 7-4. Common vent arrangements.

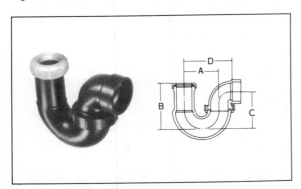

Fig. 7-5. An adjustable trap fitting, constructed from ABS plastic (Courtesy of Nibco).

ties into a laundry tray. Indirect venting is not allowed in most plumbing situations.

Another key part in the overall plumbing system is the traps. A trap (Fig. 7-5), is a U-shaped plumbing fitting located between the fixture and the drain or waste line. Water remains in the curve of the trap at all times, creating what is called a *trap seal*. This seal prevents sewer gases from entering the house through the fixture's drain. Traps are required on all sink, shower, and bathtub drain lines.

The horizontal pipe which extends from the trap to the soil line is called the *trap arm* (Fig. 7-6), and

Fig. 7-6. The trap and trap arm assembly under a bathroom sink. The trap arm connects to a sanitary tee fitting (right), which is in turn connected to the drain line (below) and the vent line (above).

Table 7-1. Minimum Trap and Trap Arm Sizes.

FIXTURE BEING SERVED	SIZE OF TRAP & TRAP ARM
Bathtub	1½ inches
Bidet	1½ inches
Clothes washer	2 inches
Laundry tub	1½ inches
Sink, bathroom, single	1¼ inches
Sink, bathroom, double	1½ inches
Stall shower	2 inches
Toilet*	3 inches

*Size is for trap arm only. A trap is built into the toilet itself; no in-line trap is used.

Table 7-2. Maximum Length of Trap Arms.

SIZE OF TRAP ARM	LENGTH FROM TRAP TO VENT
1¼ inches	2 feet 6 inches
1½ inches	3 feet 6 inches
2 inches	5 feet 0 inches
3 inches	6 feet 0 inches
4 inches	10 feet 0 inches

REMOVING THE PLUMBING FIXTURES

Three basic plumbing phases are involved in remodeling a bathroom: removal of the existing plumbing fixtures, (Fig. 7-7), roughing-in the new plumbing, and final top-out. Take your time to plan each phase carefully, making certain you have the proper tools and materials on hand and that you understand each of the steps you will be taking.

One task that the remodeler must face is removing the existing plumbing fixtures. If you intend to reuse or sell the fixtures, take great care in removing them, since the porcelain or fiberglass with which they are made can be damaged easily by tools or

in order for the trap and drain system to work correctly, the trap arm cannot be too long or too small. The plumbing codes specify the minimum size of the pipe used for a trap arm, and also the maximum length it can be. Examples of these sizes are shown in Tables 7-1 & 7-2, but you should always verify your pipe sizes and plumbing layout with the building department prior to commencing work.

Fig. 7-7. Old threaded galvanized water and waste lines, prior to removal and relocation. In rooms where a lot of under-floor plumbing work needs to be done, you'll often find it easier and faster to simply remove a section of the floor to gain access to the pipes.

rough handling. Stops, supply lines, and toilet bolts, though reusable, should be discarded in most cases. These parts are inexpensive, and replacing them as part of your overall remodeling project can save you problems later.

Removing Toilets

First, shut off the water to the toilet by closing the stop, then disconnect the supply line either at the stop or at the toilet. Flush the toilet several times to remove as much water as possible, then remove the remainder with a small cup.

There are two bolts that hold the toilet to the flange. (Some older toilets have four bolts—two in the flange and two that go into the floor.) Remove the caps that cover the bolts by prying up on them, then use a wrench to remove the nuts from the bolts. If the nuts have rusted closed, it will be necessary to cut them off with a hacksaw.

With the supply line and nuts removed, the toilet is ready to come up. Rock it gently from side to side to break the wax seal then, with a helper, lift it straight up and off the bolts. Clean any left over wax off the floor flange, and also off the bottom of the toilet if it is going to be reused.

Removing Sinks and Faucets

Close the stops and unhook the water lines first; you will find it easier to disconnect the lines at the stops rather than at the faucet. Next, using a pipe wrench, spud wrench, or large adjustable pliers, loosen the two large nuts on either end of the trap. Place a bucket under the trap to catch the water, then remove the trap.

You should take a moment to study the existing sink installation. Some types are set down with adhesive, and simply need to be pried up. Others are held in place from underneath with screws and clips (Fig. 7-8); loosen the screws, remove the clips, then pry up the sink. A third possibility is that the sink was tiled into place, in which case you will need to use a hammer and cold chisel to carefully remove the tiles that hold the sink. When chipping tile, always wear goggles and gloves.

Wall-mounted sinks hang from a large wall bracket; simply lift the sink straight up and off the bracket, then unscrew and remove the bracket itself. For a pedestal sink, first check to see if the sink and pedestal are in two pieces. If they are, remove the sink from the pedestal first (there might be a bolt holding the two together). Finally, remove the bolts (if any) that hold the pedestal to the floor.

If the sink and counter are one piece, it was either installed with adhesive or with screws from underneath. If the backsplash is a separate piece, pry it off first. Then, remove the screws or clips, if any. Finally, lift or gently pry up the counter to separate it from the cabinet.

Removing Bathtubs and Showers

To remove a bathtub, you will first need to disconnect all of its plumbing. Begin by removing the

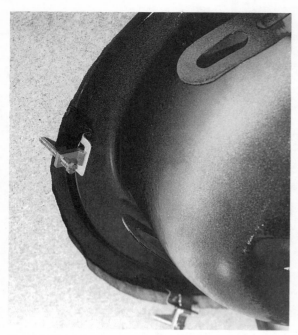

Fig. 7-8. The clip and screw arrangement used to secure a bathroom sink to the countertop.

tub filler spout and faucet handles, plus any trim rings. Leave the faucet stems stubbed out of the wall. Next, remove the screws that hold the overflow plate and drain lever in place (if there is one), and pull out the lift linkage. Remove the stopper mechanism in the tub drain. From underneath, disconnect the nuts that hold the drain line and trap in place.

Next you will need to remove all or part of the material on the walls surrounding the tub. If full panels of fiberglass or other material cover the wall, pry them off and remove them completely. If the walls are tiled, remove at least a 6 inch strip of tile all around the tub (or remove all the tile, since you'll have a very difficult time trying to patch it with new material). If there is only drywall on the walls, remove a 6-inch-wide strip on all three sides of the tub. You will have exposed the tub's flange and the part of the wall studs.

If the tub flange has been screwed to the studs, remove the screws. The tub is ready now to be removed. If it is a fiberglass unit, simply lift it up and out, away from the walls, then carry it out of the

room. Cast-iron and steel tubs are a little more difficult, and definitely require two people. The easiest method is to place two 2 × 4's in front of the tub and perpendicular to it, then lift the tub up while pulling forward, so that the tub rests on the boards. Slide it the rest of the way out onto the boards, which will enable you to reach under it and lift it up. Remember that cast-iron tubs can weigh 200 pounds or more, so plan your route out of the house beforehand, and use care in maneuvering the tub.

For showers, the first step is to remove the faucet handles and trim rings, then disconnect the trap and drain line from underneath. If the existing shower is a one-piece fiberglass unit, the next step is to cut the drywall back around the entire perimeter of the shower, exposing the flange. Then, use a small pry bar behind the flanges to work them away from the studs, and remove the fasteners. The entire unit then can be lifted out intact. However, if you do not have door or window openings that are large enough to allow you to carry the unit out as a whole, you might be forced to break it up.

If the shower is made of ceramic tile, your only choice is to break it up and pry it off the wall in pieces (be sure to wear gloves and goggles). Once you have removed the tile, you can pry the shower pan up and remove it also.

PLUMBING MATERIALS

With the old fixtures removed, and with some of the drywall removed also, you can determine what type pipes were originally used in the construction of your house. Depending on how extensive your remodeling work is, you might wish to stay with the same material or transition to a new material. It helps to familiarize yourself with some of the more common materials on the market so that you can make the best choices for your situation.

WATER PIPES AND FITTINGS

If your bathroom is old enough to be remodeled, chances are the water lines were plumbed with galvanized threaded metal pipe. (See Fig. 7-9.) This type of pipe is still widely used today, and if your plumbing changes are relatively minor, you might

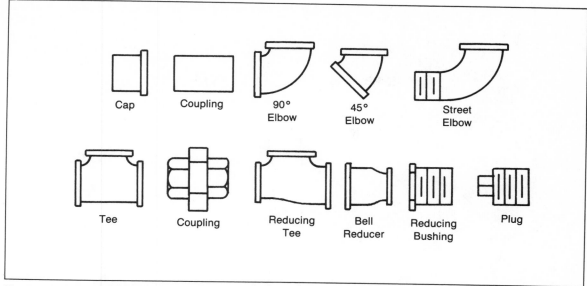

Fig. 7-9. Common threaded fittings for use with galvanized threaded pipe.

wish to stay with it. If you have a lot of plumbing to do, however, you will find that threaded pipe is difficult with which to work, requires special cutting and threading tools you will need to rent, and is fairly expensive. For these reasons, you are better off transitioning from the threaded pipe to something else. If you decide to change to a different type pipe, you will have two basic choices, copper or plastic.

Copper Pipe

Copper pipe is the material that is used most today, both in new construction and remodeling, and it is the first choice of most professionals. It is light weight, rigid, resistant to corrosion, relatively inexpensive, and easy to cut and join. A tremendous variety of reliable valves, stops, and fittings are available (Fig. 7-10), which greatly simplifies installation.

Plastic Pipe

The use of plastic pipe for water lines has been growing slowly and steadily over the last several years, particularly in the construction of mobile homes. However, it still represents only a small portion of the pipe used in residential construction.

Plastic offers the advantage of being quick and easy to join, and some types are flexible enough to

be bent around obstacles without the use of extra fittings. Fitting choices are limited compared to copper, however, and some of the plastic valves and stops on the market are of poor quality and are not very reliable. If you choose to use plastic pipe, you need to be aware of the different types used for water lines in order to select the appropriate one for your job. Some common plastic pipe types and their uses are shown in Table 7-3.

WORKING WITH COPPER PIPE AND FITTINGS

The one thing about copper pipe that scares off many do-it-yourselfers is the fact that it is joined by soldering. Soldering copper is a very simple procedure, however, and can be learned in just a few minutes. You might wish to practice with some scrap pipe and fittings to get the feel of it before starting on the bathroom plumbing.

Copper can be cut to length with a fine-toothed hacksaw, but since the pipe is relatively soft, there is a risk of applying too much pressure with the saw and deforming the cut end. For that reason, the use of a tubing cutter is recommended. (See Figs. 7-11 & 7-12.) Simply place the cutter on the pipe, tighten the handle to bring the cutting wheel into contact

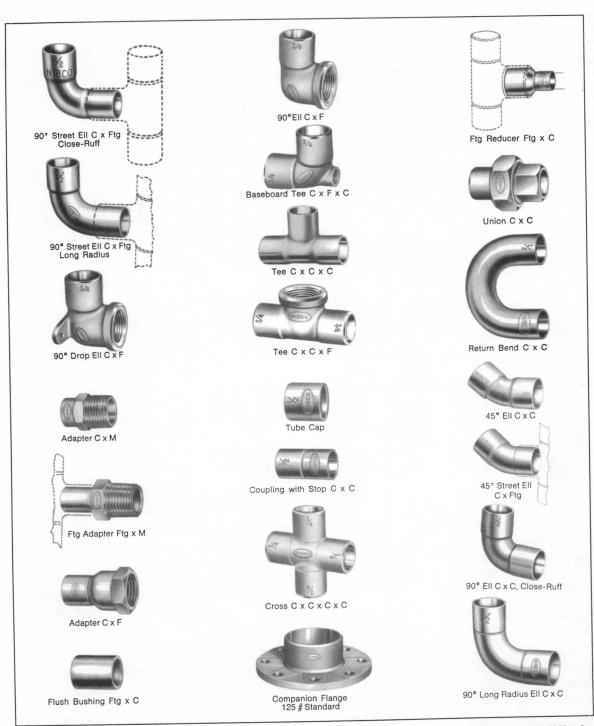

90° Street Ell C x Ftg
Close-Ruff

90° Street Ell C x Ftg
Long Radius

90° Drop Ell C x F

Adapter C x M

Ftg Adapter Ftg x M

Adapter C x F

Flush Bushing Ftg x C

90° Ell C x F

Baseboard Tee C x F x C

Tee C x C x C

Tee C x C x F

Tube Cap

Coupling with Stop C x C

Cross C x C x C x C

Companion Flange
125 # Standard

Ftg Reducer Ftg x C

Union C x C

Return Bend C x C

45° Ell C x C

45° Street Ell
C x Ftg

90° Ell C x C, Close-Ruff

90° Long Radius Ell C x C

Fig. 7-10. A sample of some of the many types and sizes of fittings available for use with copper pipe (Courtesy of Nibco).

106

Table 7-3. Common Types of Plastic Pipe.

COMMON NAME	CHEMICAL NAME	TYPE AND USES
ABS	acrylonitrile butadiene styrene	A rigid, black plastic pipe, very widely used for drain, waste, and vent (DWV) systems
CPVC	chlorinated polyvinyl chloride	Similar to PVC, but also suitable for use with hot water
PB	polybutylene	One of the most common plastic pipes for water lines, it is flexible and suitable for both hot and cold water
PE	polyethylene	A flexible plastic tubing for cold water lines
PP	polypropylene	A rigid plastic pipe used primarily for making traps and drainlines
PVC	polyvinyl chloride	A rigid plastic pipe used in some cold water applications, and also used for DWV lines
SR	styrene rubber	A rigid pipe used primarily underground

with the pipe, then rotate the cutter, tightening the handle with each revolution until the pipe comes apart.

To join copper pipe, you will need a propane torch, 50/50 solder, flux and flux brush, sandpaper, emery cloth, or a wire brush made for use with copper pipe and fittings. You can purchase all these tools and materials at your plumbing supply dealer or a hardware store. If you have a number of joints to solder, you might wish to use one of the bottled high-heat gases instead of regular propane, which will work with the same torch head.

The key to soldering is a clean joint. Using the sandpaper, emery cloth, or wire brush, clean the end of the pipe (at least to the depth that it will go into the fitting) and the inside of the fitting until they are shining. (See Fig. 7-13.) Coat the end of the pipe with flux (Fig. 7-14), and insert the pipe into the fitting. Align the fitting in the direction you want it, then apply heat to the joint. (See Fig. 7-15.) The copper will begin to discolor slightly as it heats, which is an indicator of when to apply the solder.

When you heat the joint withdraw the flame and touch the end of the solder to the joint. If the joint is hot enough, it will quickly suck the solder into it. If it does not, apply more heat. If, after two or three

tries, the joint will not take the solder, let it cool, remove the fitting from the pipe, and clean and flux both of them again.

When soldering a run of pipe, it is best to solder pipe into all the openings of a fitting at the same time. This method prevents the heat from loosening an already soldered joint. If soldering both ends of a fitting at the same time isn't possible, wrap the already soldered end with a damp cloth to prevent it from heating up. If you need to disassemble a joint, simply heat it until the solder flows, then pull the joint apart with two pairs of pliers.

DWV PIPES AND FITTINGS

For your drain, waste, and vent lines, including the main soil pipes, your house might have been plumbed originally with any one of a variety of materials. Probably the most common soil pipe in older homes was cast iron, laboriously cut with special chain cutters, then assembled using oakem and molten lead. Cast iron was used also for larger vent stacks, while threaded pipe was used often for smaller vents.

Cast-iron pipe is still regularly used today, although band clamps (also called no-hub clamps), have

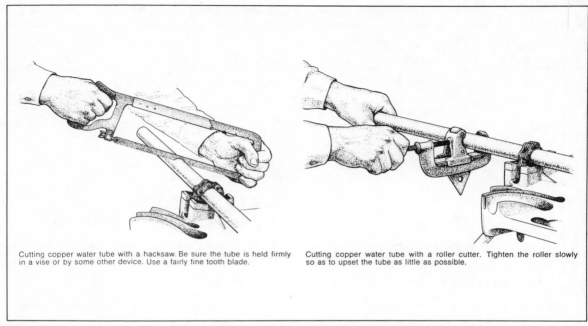

Cutting copper water tube with a hacksaw. Be sure the tube is held firmly in a vise or by some other device. Use a fairly fine tooth blade.

Cutting copper water tube with a roller cutter. Tighten the roller slowly so as to upset the tube as little as possible.

Fig. 7-11. Using a hacksaw (left) and a tubing cutter (right) to cut copper pipe (Courtesy of Nibco).

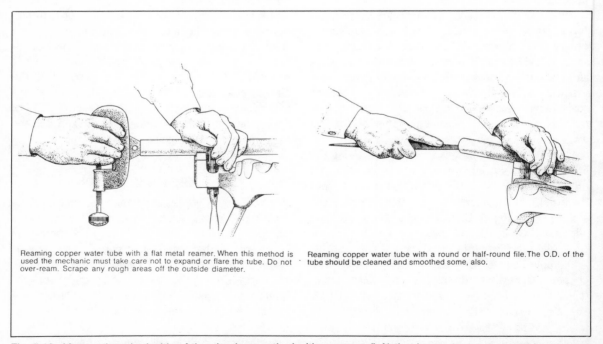

Reaming copper water tube with a flat metal reamer. When this method is used the mechanic must take care not to expand or flare the tube. Do not over-ream. Scrape any rough areas off the outside diameter.

Reaming copper water tube with a round or half-round file. The O.D. of the tube should be cleaned and smoothed some, also.

Fig. 7-12. After cutting, the inside of the pipe is smoothed with a reamer (left) that is attached to most tubing cutters. An alternate method is to use a round file (right) (Courtesy of Nibco).

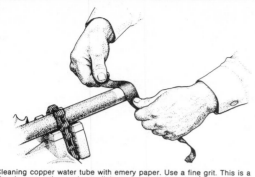

Cleaning copper water tube with emery paper. Use a fine grit. This is a cleaning operation and very little surface needs to be removed.

Cleaning a copper fitting with emery paper. Be sure to clean the bottom of the socket or cup.

Cleaning a copper fitting with a wire brush. Powered wire brushes are available for use when enough fittings are being cleaned to make a power unit economical.

Fig. 7-13. Using emery cloth (top and center) and a wire fitting brush (bottom) to clean the pipe and fitting prior to assembly (Courtesy of Nibco).

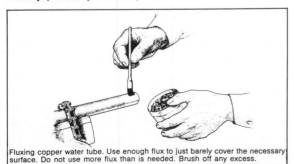

Fluxing copper water tube. Use enough flux to just barely cover the necessary surface. Do not use more flux than is needed. Brush off any excess.

Fig. 7-14. Applying a paste flux to the end of the pipe (Courtesy of Nibco).

Heating copper water tube. The tube is heated first, momentarily, so that the heat will transfer to the end of the tube. Point the flame slightly away from the fitting.

Heating a copper fitting. Be careful not to overheat. Use enough heat, but no more than enough.

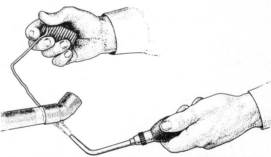

Applying solder to the heated joint. Do not melt the solder with the torch. Get the joint to the proper temperature and melt the solder by touching it to the tube-fitting juncture with a gently pushing movement.

Solder joints can be wiped with a clean cloth, while they are still hot, to make them even smoother and more attractive. If it is necessary to cool them quickly the cloth can be damp.

Fig. 7-15. The proper method for heating and soldering copper pipe (Courtesy of Nibco).

replaced the old hand-poured molten lead seals. Cast iron is required by some plumbing codes for use where a soil line passes under a foundation. Another common use is for second floor soil lines when they pass through living space. The sound of running water is not nearly as loud through cast iron as it is through plastic pipe.

In the case of most DWV pipes installed today, however, plastic is the overwhelming choice. While PVC is used occasionally, especially for septic system drain fields, ABS (acrylonitrile butadiene styrene) pipe and fittings are the most common. ABS pipe is a strong, light weight, and relatively inexpensive black plastic material, commonly available in 1½, 2, 3, and 4 inch sizes. A wide variety of compatible fittings is also available.

WORKING WITH ABS PIPE AND FITTINGS

The real joy of ABS pipe is how easy it is to use. (See Fig. 7-16.) The pipe is cut to length with a hacksaw or fine-toothed handsaw, such as a backsaw. Take care that the cut is straight; if desired, a miter box can be used. Clean away any burrs on the end of the pipe prior to assembly, and make sure the pipe and fittings are clean.

Test-fit the pipe and fittings with "dry assembly" before gluing to make certain they are the right length and properly aligned. You will have very little time to work with them once they are glued. Disassemble the joint, and apply a coating of ABS cement to both the end of the pipe and the inside of the fitting. Press the pipe fully into the fitting with a twisting motion, align it, and hold it until it sets. Work quickly, as the glue sets in a matter of seconds. Wipe off excess glue with a rag.

Use a scrap of wood or cardboard to protect floors and other surfaces from glue drips, and wear light cotton gloves to keep it off your hands. Lacquer thinner will remove excess ABS cement from most surfaces, including your hands, but use it sparingly.

TRANSITIONS
BETWEEN DISSIMILAR MATERIALS

One area of particular importance is the proper transition between dissimilar materials. This situation arises quite often in remodeling, where it becomes necessary or desirable to adapt copper pipe to threaded metal, or ABS to cast iron or other types of soil pipe. These situations are so common, in fact, that specific fittings to make these transitions easy and fool-proof commonly are available at plumbing supply stores.

Adapting Copper Pipe
to Galvanized Metal Pipe

Copper pipes and galvanized metal pipes cannot be joined directly to each. The zinc used in the galvanizing process is not compatible with copper; when the two come into contact with each other, a corrosive chemical reaction begins that, over time, will eat away at the joint and cause it to fail.

The proper way to make the transition is through the use of a special fitting, called a *dielectric union*. (See Fig. 7-17.) The union has a slip fitting on one end for direct soldering to copper pipe. The other end is threaded for attachment to the galvanized pipe. In between the two ends are rubber and plastic washers which keep the metals apart. Use of the dielectric union, which is required by the plumbing codes, ensures a leak- and corrosion-proof joint, and also provides you with a convenient method of assembly and disassembly where the pipes join.

Adapting ABS Pipe to Cast-Iron Pipe

To adapt ABS pipe to cast iron, or any other material, a band clamp is used. (See Fig. 7-18.) The clamp consists of a metal sleeve with a worm-drive clamp at each end. Inside the metal sleeve is a thick rubber sleeve with two different inside diameters, one that fits the ABS pipe and one that fits the cast iron. Interchangeable rubber sleeves with different inside diameters can be used when adapting ABS to clay, transite, or other types of pipe. Your dealer can show you the proper one to use.

To install the band clamp, slip the metal and rubber sleeves over one of the pipes. Work the rubber sleeve forward onto the other pipe until it is centered over both. Finally, move the metal sleeve into position over the rubber sleeve, and secure the clamp by tightening the worm-drive clamps.

1. Begin by cutting the pipe. Use a miter box or tube cutter with a blade for plastic. Make sure the end is square so that the pipe will seat correctly in the fitting and the joint will be strong.

2. Next, smooth the end of the pipe. Use a pocket knife, file, or special deburring tool to slightly level edges that might scrape away the solvent during the bonding process.

3. Then, to check for interference fit, insert the pipe into the fitting. It should not go all the way into the seat of the fitting at this time.

4. Now you are ready to apply the primer, if you are working with CPVC or PVC. (Primer is not required for ABS.) Be sure the surfaces are clean and dry. Apply primer first to the inside of the fitting, then to the outside of the pipe, as far up as you will need to accommodate the fitting when it is in place. Be careful not to leave a puddle in the bottom of the fitting. Wait five to 15 seconds before applying solvent.

5. Apply the proper solvent cement. While the surfaces are still wet from the primer, brush a full, even coat of solvent cement onto the inside of the fitting. Again, be careful not to form a puddle in the bottom of the fitting. (Applying too heavy a coat or leaving a puddle will result in some flow restriction.) Next, apply solvent to the pipe to the same level as you applied primer.

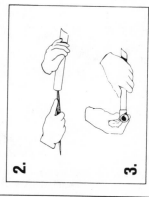

6. Now insert the pipe into the fitting immediately, before the solvent evaporates. Use enough force to ensure that the pipe bottoms in the fitting socket. Give the fitting about a quarter turn as you push it

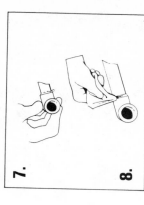

on; this will assure even distribution and absorption of the solvent. Then hold the joint firmly for about 10 seconds (longer in cold weather) to allow the solvent to start bonding the two surfaces. If you position and release too soon, the interference fit will force the pipe out. The edges of NIBCO fittings are marked in eighths to help you with alignment and positioning.

7. Check the bead of cement that has been pushed out during the assembly and alignment. A properly made joint will have a ring of cement all the way around the joint.

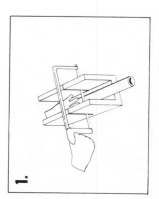

8. Wipe off the excess cement with a clean rag, leaving an even fillet all the way around. This helps the joint cure faster.

Fig. 7-16. The steps involved in properly joining ABS or PVC plastic pipe and fittings (Courtesy of Nibco).

Fig. 7-17. Dielectric unions used to adapt new runs of copper pipe to existing hot and cold threaded pipes.

Fig. 7-18. A band clamp (center) used to adapt a new 2-inch ABS waste line to the existing 4-inch cast-iron pipes. The cast iron is first cut with a chain cutter, leaving about a 4-inch stub to which the band clamp is attached. A short length of 4-inch ABS is inserted into the other end of the clamp, followed by a 4- × 2-inch bushing which receives the new 2-inch ABS pipe.

ABS pipe also can be joined directly to threaded metal pipe. If the metal pipe has been cut and does not have a threaded end, the connection is made with a band clamp having the appropriate inner rubber sleeve.

If the metal pipe is threaded, simply use an ABS female (inside thread)-to-slip fitting. Apply Teflon tape to the threads of the metal pipe (do not use regular pipe joint compound, as many types will eat away at the plastic fitting), screw the fitting firmly onto it, then glue the ABS pipe into the other end. For adapting to a threaded metal fitting, male (outside thread)-to-slip fittings commonly are available.

If you encounter an older cast-iron hub fitting, you can adapt ABS pipe to that also. (See Fig. 7-19.) Begin with a 10- or 12-inch length of threaded metal pipe that is the same inside diameter as the cast-iron pipe. When you insert the metal pipe into the cast-iron fitting, you will notice a large gap between the fitting and the pipe. Insert a length of oakem into the gap, packing it down tightly while keeping the pipe centered in the fitting. Finish the joint with a length of lead wool, which is packed tightly into the gap with a hammer and cold chisel or similar tool. Oakem and lead wool are available at plumbing supply stores.

ROUGHING-IN THE NEW PLUMBING

The pipes that are contained within the walls, under the floor, or in the attic are referred to as the *rough plumbing* (Fig. 7-20), and the process of installing them is known as *roughing-in*. The roughing-in phase is critically important—most of the pipes you install at this stage later will be concealed within the walls, so they need to be correctly installed, properly positioned to accept the new fixtures, and, of course, free of any leaks.

If your bathroom is new, you will need to extend hot and cold water lines to the bathroom's location, as well as a new branch of the main soil line. All of the new plumbing then will be tied into these

Fig. 7-19. Adapting 2-inch ABS pipe to an existing 2-inch cast-iron hub. A new, 8-inch length of threaded pipe was inserted into the hub, then sealed with oakum and lead wool. From there it's simply a matter of installing a slip x female thread adapter to the end of the threaded pipe, then gluing the new ABS run into the fitting. The white band to the right of the ABS fitting is Teflon tape, which was used to seal the threads. Do not use regular pipe joint compound on ABS or PVC, as it can deteriorate the plastic.

Fig. 7-20. Rough plumbing for a new toilet, including the soil and water lines, installed between the second floor joists.

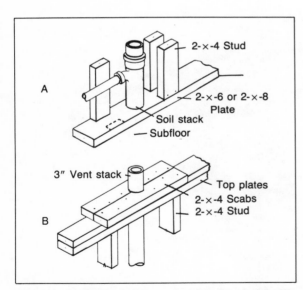

Fig. 7-21. Doubled 2 × 4s on a 2- × -6 or 2- × -8 plate (A), used to construct a wet wall that better accommodates large diameter soil lines. When a wet wall is not used and a large portion of the 2- × -4 plate is cut away to receive a 3-inch pipe (B), the plates need to be reinforced with 2- × -4 blocking.

pipes. To maintain good water pressure in the new bathroom, you should plan on using ¾-inch pipe to bring the hot and cold water lines to the room, then you can take ½-inch lines off of those to supply the fixtures. You also will need to plan on a 3- or 4-inch soil line.

Here is where you will want to refer back to the map of the plumbing system you made earlier, which will allow you to select the best location for tying the new plumbing into the old plumbing. Ideally, you want to select a spot that is accessible for you to work on, that has fittings that can easily be disassembled and tied into, and in the case of the new soil line, that is low enough to provide the proper fall.

With an existing bathroom that is being remodeled, a lot depends on how extensive your fixture location changes are. If all the fixtures are to be in the same location as they were previously, chances are very little rough plumbing needs to be done. When the fixture locations are changed, however, you will need to make plumbing changes also.

Wet Walls

Prior to roughing-in your plumbing, you might find it advantageous to construct a *wet wall*, which is simply a wall with greater interior depth to better accommodate all the plumbing. Wet walls are especially helpful, and in some cases essential, when two bathrooms are back to back and the plumbing for both will be placed in the same wall.

A wet wall can be built in a number of different ways (Fig. 7-21), depending on your particular plumbing situation and how much floor space you have available:

☐ Use 2-×-6 or 2-×-8 material and place the studs 24 inches on center
☐ Use 2-×-6 or 2-×-8 plates, then place two rows of 2-×-4 studs with the 3 ½-inch side facing out
☐ Build two 2-×-4 walls, spaced apart as far as necessary
☐ Fur out an existing 2-×-4 wall with additional material to create greater depth

General Rough-In Guidelines

During rough-in, you will want to extend the pipes up (or down) into the walls, then out into the room to a point where they will be visible and accessible after the walls have been covered. (See Fig. 7-22.) Water lines need to be capped off so that the water to the house can be turned back on. Drain and waste lines should be capped also either with glue-on caps or with reusable rubber plugs. The floor flange for the toilet (Fig. 7-23), usually has a plastic cover already in place, or you can use a rubber plug.

Rough-in dimensions have become somewhat standardized over the years, and the following ones are common for most types of fixtures. Before beginning, however, check with your plumbing supplier to verify the rough-in locations for the specific fixtures you are buying. You will want to check with

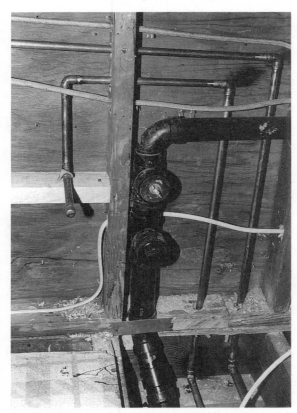

Fig. 7-22. Water and waste lines roughed-in for a new sink and set so as to extend out through the finished wall. Note the cleanout fitting and plug on the soil line (lower right) and the temporary plug used to seal the waste line fitting (upper right) until the trap arm can be installed.

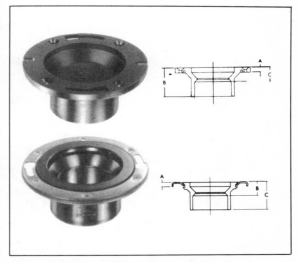

Fig. 7-23. Common ABS closet flanges. The upper one (A) has a built-in plastic plug that seals the line until the toilet is installed. The four countersunk holes receive flat head screws to hold the flange against the floor, and the toilet bolts can be placed in the two small openings (left and right) or the larger slots (front and back). The lower flange (B) has a rotating ring that simplifies alignment of the bolts (Courtesy of Nibco).

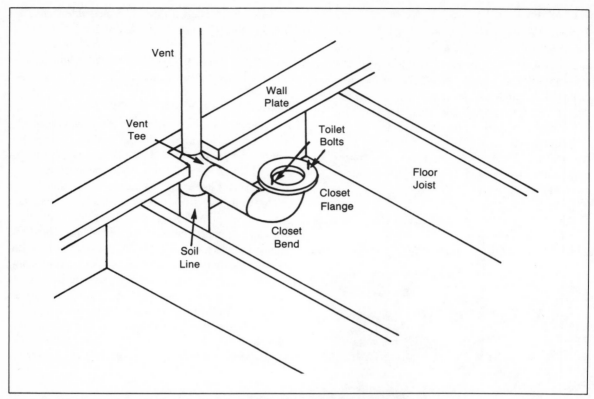

Fig. 7-24. The common method of roughing-in the soil and vent lines for a toilet.

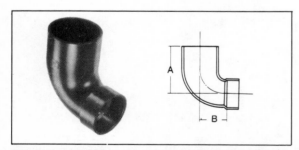

Fig. 7-25. An ABS closet bend fitting (Courtesy of Nibco).

the local building department to see if any special plumbing codes are in effect in your area, and to check on the size and layout of the waste and vent lines you will be using.

Roughing-In Toilets

The toilet is usually the fixture that will give you the most trouble at the rough-in stage. Each toilet must have its own 2-inch vent (Fig. 7-24), although other fixtures can be back vented into the toilet vent at a higher level. A 3-inch waste line is also required, and the toilet must be down-stream from any sink, bathtub, or shower that shares the same line. Most plumbers will try to place the waste lines for the toilet first, then lay out other fixture locations.

First, you should install the closet flange and closet bend (Fig. 7-25), between the floor joists. The closet flange must be placed carefully so that its height will be level with the finished floor, and so that the slots in the top lip which accommodate the toilet bolts are on the sides, not in front and back. The center of the flange should be 12 inches out from the finished wall surface (Fig. 7-26), (be sure to allow for the thickness of the wall finish material). Most plumbers will increase that dimension to 12¼ inches from the finished wall to simplify installation. If desired, and if the closet flange is drilled for them,

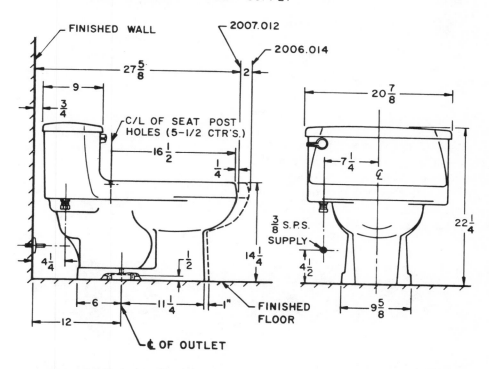

LEXINGTON TOILET 2006.014
VITREOUS CHINA—ONE PIECE
SHOWN WITH 3/8 FLEX. SUPPLY

2007.012

PLUMBER NOTE: THIS COMBINATION IS DESIGNED TO ROUGH-IN AT A MINIMUM DIMENSION OF 12" FROM FINISHED WALL TO C/L OF OUTLET.

DIMENSIONS SHOWN FOR SUPPLY ARE SUGGESTED

NOTE: 3/8 SUPPLY NOT INCLUDED WITH FIXTURE AND MUST BE ORDERED SEPARATELY.

IMPORTANT: Dimensions of fixtures are nominal and may vary within the range of tolerances established by ANSI Standards A112.19.2.

These measurements are subject to change or cancellation. No responsibility is assumed for use of superseded or voided leaflets.

AMERICAN STANDARD

T288

88

JAN. 1981

Fig. 7-26. Rough-in dimensions for a floor-mounted toilet (Courtesy of American Standard).

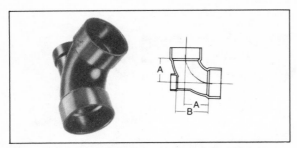

Fig. 7-27. A special ABS toilet fitting that connects the incoming soil line, the outgoing soil line, and the vent line (Courtesy of Nibco).

flathead wood screws can be used to secure the flange to the floor.

A special toilet fitting (Fig. 7-27), is used commonly at the wall, which has a 3-inch inlet for the pipe coming from the closet bend, a 3-inch outlet on the bottom for the pipe leading to the soil line, and a 2-inch outlet on top for the vent line. No separate trap is required, since there is already one built into the toilet.

The toilet also requires a single ½-inch cold-water line (Fig. 7-28), which usually is stubbed out of the wall about 8 inches up from the floor. If you are using one of the low, one-piece toilets, the stub-out must be lower on the wall, about 3 inches up, or come up through the floor.

Roughing-In Bidets

A bidet is plumbed more like a shower than a toilet. (See Fig. 7-29.) Extend a 1½- or 2-inch line to the bidet's location, then install a trap. Next, bring hot- and cold-water lines up into the wall behind the bidet, approximately 4 inches off the floor and 4 inches to either side of center. Refer to the manufacturer's recommendations for complete instructions.

Roughing-In Sinks

A bathroom sink requires a 1½-inch drain line and a 1½-inch vent. Use a sanitary tee fitting in the wall, which allows a 1½-inch outlet for the drain and

Fig. 7-28. A typical completed rough-in. The two ABS lines at left are for a downstairs vent (left) and for the new upstairs sink (right). The two copper water lines are for the new sink. The plumbing group at right includes an ABS vent from downstairs (left) and an ABS vent and copper water line for the new upstairs toilet (right). The closet flange with a temporary rubber plug can be seen just forward of the pipes.

C-1. (above) A room on the third floor of a 1910-era mansion converted to a master bath (below) provides space for a luxurious tub and separate compartment for toilet and bidet. Shades of Heather and Shell ceramic tile flow from the floor to the set-up tub, into the frosted-glass-doored compartment and the matching Heather pedestal sink.

C-2. (above) The coolness of a rain forest was achieved in this master bath by the synthetic marble used for the floor and vanities, and the hand-painted foliage and chrome-plated leaves on the walls. ''Mirror-image'' vanities and sinks allow the room to be used by two people at once, while maintaining privacy. The alcove holds a whirlpool bathtub, with a separate shower stall adjacent. (below) Deep blue fixtures, sand-colored tile, and brass give this room a masculine look. The black shelving and the fireplace give the room a feeling of luxury.

C-3. (above) Rustic charm in a small space defines this bath. The moldings and false exposed beams have a weathered look. The sheet flooring was wrapped up the walls. (below) This bath reflects the home's beachfront site. Low-maintenance ceramic tile and plastic laminates were used. The color scheme gives the room a soft glow, like driftwood. (Courtesy of Kohler Company)

C-10. The warmth of wood and traditional detailing set this turn-of-the-century re-creation apart from ordinary bathrooms. Heavy wood moldings and reproduction light fixtures set the room off, and the colors have been carefully coordinated, right down to the artwork and the towels. (Courtesy of Kohler Company)

C-11. A beautiful, hand-laid mosaic of ceramic tile gives this bathroom an individual look. The floor is at different levels to break the room up into separate areas, and the steps are highlighted by more inlaid ceramic tile. Ample storage is provided by the open, ceramic-tiled shelves at right. (Courtesy of American Olean Tile)

C-12. (top) For the ultimate in bathroom relaxation, the Environment Masterbath™ from Kohler is definitely the answer. The self-contained unit starts with a two-person whirlpool bathtub beneath a padded deck, enclosed in a teakwood interior. Added to that is the unit's ability to artifically re-create a variety of nature's soothing climatic conditions: sauna, steam, sun, wind, and gentle rain. (Courtesy of Kohler Company)

(left) A sauna at the end of the day can be a reality in your new bathroom. Many smaller, affordable models in do-it-yourself kits are being offered by different manufacturers, and can be incorporated into many bathroom layouts with relative ease. (Courtesy of Tylo Saunas)

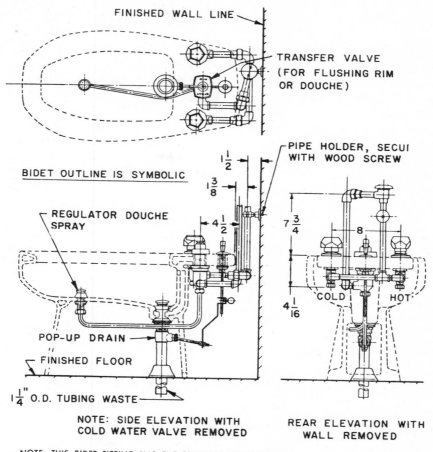

Bidet Fittings

3325.SER.

Fixture Mounted

FINISHED WALL LINE

TRANSFER VALVE
(FOR FLUSHING RIM
OR DOUCHE)

PIPE HOLDER, SECUI
WITH WOOD SCREW

BIDET OUTLINE IS SYMBOLIC

REGULATOR DOUCHE
SPRAY

$1\frac{1}{2}$

$1\frac{3}{8}$

$4\frac{1}{2}$

$7\frac{3}{4}$

8

$4\frac{1}{16}$

COLD   HOT

POP-UP DRAIN

FINISHED FLOOR

$1\frac{1}{4}"$ O.D. TUBING WASTE

NOTE: SIDE ELEVATION WITH
COLD WATER VALVE REMOVED

REAR ELEVATION WITH
WALL REMOVED

NOTE: THIS BIDET FITTING HAS THE TRANSFER VALVE FEATURE

NOTE:
PROVISION MUST BE MADE FOR THE INSTALLATION OF TRAP IN, FLOOR (FOR THRU THE
FLOOR OUTLET APPLICATION)

IMPORTANT:

These measurements are subject to change or cancellation. No responsibility is
assumed for use of superseded or voided leaflets.

AMERICAN STANDARD

BF001

86

MAY, 1979

Fig. 7-29. Details of the rough-in dimensions and plumbing fittings used for installing a bidet (Courtesy of American Standard).

vent lines and a 1½-inch inlet from the sink. The drain outlet should be approximately 16 inches up from the floor, and should be fairly well centered to the new sink. If you are using double sinks, the outlet should be centered to either one of the sinks, or centered between them. The trap is installed during top-out, and can be used to make the final alignment.

You will need ½-inch hot- and cold-water lines. Ideally, the cold water pipe should come up on the right side of the drain line, and the hot water pipe on the left of the drain. If this is not possible, both pipes can come up on the same side of the drain line, always with the cold to the right of the hot. The pipes can come up in the wall and elbow out under the sink (Fig. 7-30), which is the preferred installation, or they can come directly up through the floor. Plan on stubbing the pipes out about 20 inches above the floor and 4 inches on either side of the drain. (See Fig. 7-31.) You can plumb widely-spaced double sinks with two drain lines in the wall (Figs. 7-32 & 7-33); you can hook closely-spaced sinks together into a single drain during top-out.

Roughing-In Bathtubs, Stall Showers, and Tub/Shower Combinations

If the bathtub you have purchased has a left- or right-hand drain outlet (something that is determined beforehand and specified when ordering), then that determines which wall will house the plumbing. With a stall shower, the outlet is usually in the center of the shower pan.

Tubs and showers drain through a trap and drain line, which are placed under the floor during the rough-in stage. If the trap will be concealed between second floor joists (Fig. 7-33), it should be a fixed trap as shown. If it will be exposed in a crawl space or basement, the trap should be removable. The drain line runs to a branch drain or soil line, and then is back-vented or wet-vented. A 12-inch-square hole (Fig. 7-34), is cut usually in the floor above the trap, which allows the necessary movement and clearance for connecting it to the fixture.

Bathtubs and stall showers commonly are set in place during the rough-in stage also, which allows you to install the drywall around them. For bathtubs, purchase a standard bathtub waste and overflow kit

Fig. 7-30. A drain line fitting with temporary plastic cap and the hot and cold water lines stubbed into a vanity cabinet.

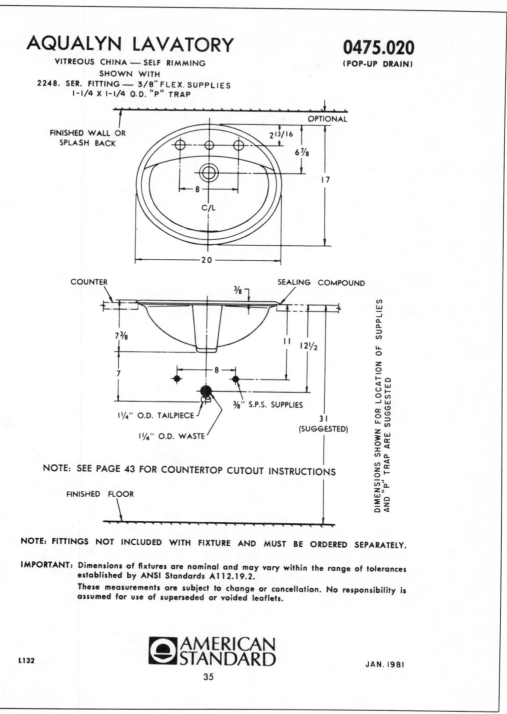

AQUALYN LAVATORY

VITREOUS CHINA — SELF RIMMING
SHOWN WITH
2248. SER. FITTING — 3/8" FLEX. SUPPLIES
1-1/4 X 1-1/4 O.D. "P" TRAP

0475.020

(POP-UP DRAIN)

OPTIONAL

FINISHED WALL OR
SPLASH BACK

2 13/16

6 7/8

17

8

C/L

20

COUNTER

SEALING COMPOUND

3/8

7 3/8

7

8

11   12 1/2

3/8" S.P.S. SUPPLIES

1 1/4" O.D. TAILPIECE

1 1/4" O.D. WASTE

31
(SUGGESTED)

DIMENSIONS SHOWN FOR LOCATION OF SUPPLIES
AND "P" TRAP ARE SUGGESTED

NOTE: SEE PAGE 43 FOR COUNTERTOP CUTOUT INSTRUCTIONS

FINISHED FLOOR

NOTE: FITTINGS NOT INCLUDED WITH FIXTURE AND MUST BE ORDERED SEPARATELY.

IMPORTANT: Dimensions of fixtures are nominal and may vary within the range of tolerances
established by ANSI Standards A112.19.2.

These measurements are subject to change or cancellation. No responsibility is
assumed for use of superseded or voided leaflets.

◉ AMERICAN STANDARD

JAN. 1981

35

Fig. 7-31. Rough-in locations for a self-rimming sink being installed in a vanity cabinet (Courtesy of American Standard).

Fig. 7-32. Drain line arrangement for a wide-spread pair of bathroom sinks. Note the two sets of water lines coming up through the floor.

Fig. 7-33. Another double sink rough-in (left), which also shows the back vent arrangement.

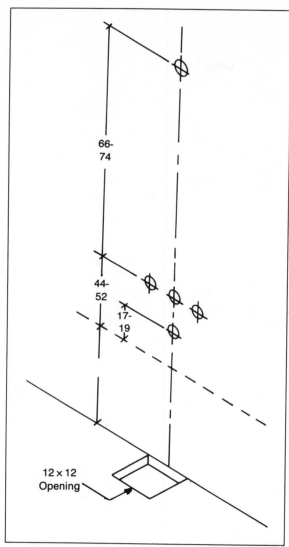

66-
74

44-
52

17-
19

12 × 12
Opening

Fig. 7-34. Typical rough-in dimensions for a bathtub/shower combination. Note the location of the square hole in the floor to accommodate the trap and waste lines.

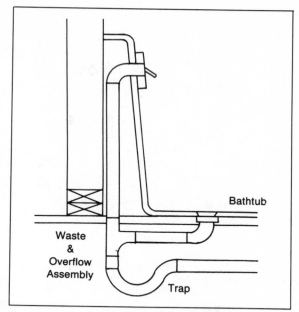

Bathtub

Waste
&
Overflow
Assembly

Trap

Fig. 7-35. A standard bathtub waste and overflow arrangement.

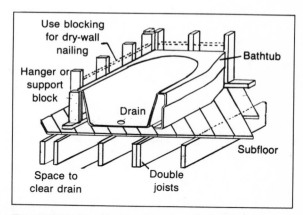

Use blocking
for dry-wall
nailing

Hanger or
support
block

Bathtub

Drain

Subfloor

Space to
clear drain

Double
joists

Fig. 7-36. Wooden blocking to support the back lip of a steel or cast-iron bathtub.

(Fig. 7-35), and install it on the tub according to the manufacturer's instructions prior to placing the tub in position. With a stall shower or shower pan, the proper drain fittings and instructions will be included.

Steel or cast-iron tubs require supports under the back ledge (Fig. 7-36), where it meets the wall. These supports can be in the form of a board nailed horizontally to the face of the studs at the proper

height, or they can be short blocks of 2 × 4 nailed to each stud.

With a helper, set the tub or shower into position so that the drain line enters the hole in the floor. Position the unit against the wall, and level and plumb it carefully. Next, if the tub, shower, or shower pan is fiberglass, you can secure it in place by nailing through the flange into the studs, or with special clips

Fig. 7-37. Special metal clips, supplied by the manufacturer, used to secure a fiberglass bathtub to the studs.

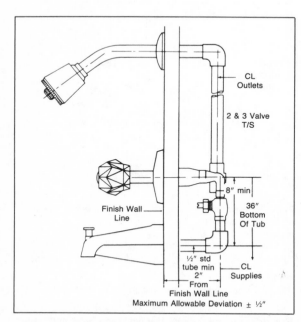

Fig. 7-38. A typical mixer valve, spout, and shower head arrangement for use with a combination tub/shower (Courtesy of Nibco).

(Fig. 7-37), provided by the manufacturer. Steel and cast-iron tubs are usually not fastened, relying instead on their own weight to keep them in place. Finally, go under the house and connect the trap to the fixtures drain line.

When installing the water lines (Fig. 7-38), you should rough the *mixer valve* (the body of the faucet) into the wall at the same time the pipes are set. (See Figs. 7-39 & 7-40.) Most installations use ½-inch water lines, but if you have an oversized bathtub or soaking tub, you might want to consider a ¾-inch faucet and water lines for faster filling.

Center the plumbing to the centerline of the tub. The outlet for the tub spout should be about 4 inches above the tub rim, and the handles should be about 16 inches above the rim. For a stall shower the handles are positioned higher on the wall, usually about 42 inches above the floor. The location of the shower head in either a stall shower or a tub/shower combination is a matter of personal preference. Common locations range from 65 to 75 inches above the floor.

TOPPING OUT THE PLUMBING

You should complete the top-out stage after the walls are covered and the flooring, cabinets and counters are in place. First, after the house water has been shut off, remove the caps and plugs from the drain and water lines.

Topping Out Toilets

If your new toilet is a two-piece model, the bowl and tank will be shipped in two separate boxes. Carefully unpack them, and immediately check them for cracks, chips or other damage. You will find a bag of thick brass screws and nuts, rubber washers,

Fig. 7-39. Using dielectric unions to tie onto the existing threaded water lines, allowing the installation of a new mixer valve body. The two vertical pipes rising above the valve are air chambers, which extend up about 12 inches and are capped. Air chambers absorb the shock of the water being shut off, preventing a banging noise in the pipes known as *water hammer.*

and other parts inside the tank; follow the manufacturer's instructions carefully and connect the tank to the bowl. One-piece toilets are shipped ready for installation.

Invert the toilet, and place a wax bowl ring over the *horn* (the round protrusion on the underside of the toilet). (See Fig. 7-41.) For best results, the wax should be warm, at least room temperature, before installing. After placing the ring over the horn, press down firmly to seal the wax. If desired, a bead of plumber's putty can be placed around the toilet's bottom edge, where it contacts the floor.

Remove the plug from the floor opening. If you have installed a new flange with a built-in plastic plug, tap the plug with a hammer until it breaks loose, then remove it. Install a new toilet bolt into each slot in the floor flange, and center them to each side of the opening. If necessary, the bolts can be held upright with a small dab of plumber's putty.

Lift the toilet into place, being certain the two holes in the base slide over the two bolts. Press the toilet down against the floor with a slight twisting motion to seal the wax. Check that the unit is level, then install the washers and nuts on the bolts. Tighten the nuts firmly with a wrench, but be careful that you don't over-tighten them and crack the bowl. Bolt covers, if supplied, can be set with plumber's putty.

Slip an escutcheon plate over the supply pipe and push it against the wall, then install an *angle stop* (a stop valve with its outlet perpendicular to its inlet) on the pipe. Use a flexible water supply line (Fig. 7-42), to connect the stop to the inlet on the underside of the tank.

Topping Out Sinks and Faucets

You will find it easiest to install the faucet on the sink prior to installation of the sink (See Fig. 7-43.) Set the faucet in place on the sink, center and align it, then secure it in place with the washers and nuts supplied with the faucet.

Bathroom faucets usually come complete with the necessary tailpiece and pop-up assembly for connecting to the sink. (See Fig. 7-44.) First, place the gasket or a bead of plumber's putty under the tailpiece flange (Fig. 7-45), then insert it into the sink

Fig. 7-40. A copper slip × male fitting (center) used to adapt a threaded valve body to nonthreaded copper pipe.

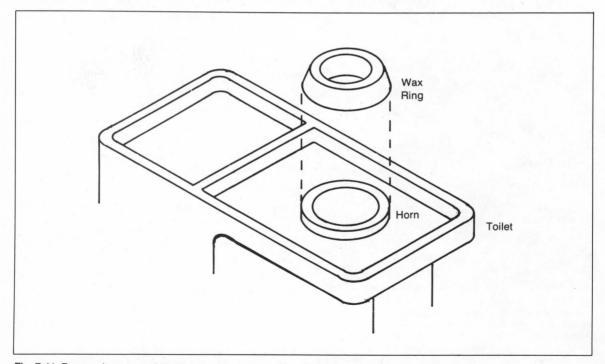

Wax Ring

Horn

Toilet

Fig. 7-41. Proper placement of the ring onto the horn on the underside of the toilet.

drain hole from above. Install the rubber and metal washers next, then secure the assembly with the nut. Follow the manufacturer's instructions and connect the pop-up assembly to the faucet and the tailpiece.

Sink installations vary depending on the type sink you are using. Some sinks are set in place with adhesive caulking, some use metal clips from under-neath, and some are an integral part of the counter and are installed in one-piece with adhesive on the cabinet and then with screws from underneath. Once again, refer to the manufacturer's recommendations for installing your particular sink.

After you have set the sink, the final step is to connect the tailpiece to the drain line using a trap. (See Fig. 7-46.) First, hold the trap in place and de-

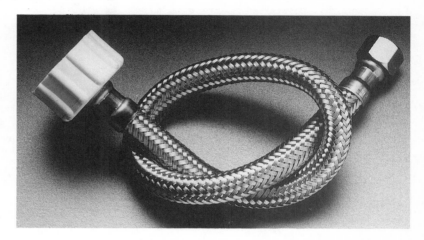

Fig. 7-42. A flexible water line for toilets, which greatly simplifies the installation, particularly when working with a low, one-piece toilet (Courtesy of Fluidmaster).

Fig. 7-43. Installation of the faucet on the sink, prior to the sink being set.

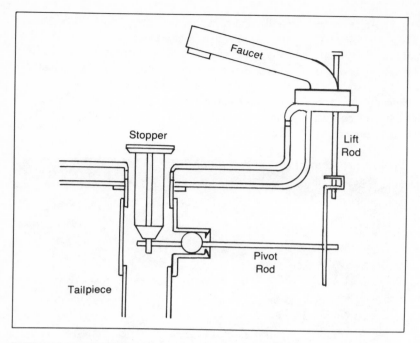

Fig. 7-44. Details of a typical tail-piece and pop-up assembly.

INSTALLATION INSTRUCTIONS
POP-UP DRAIN ASSEMBLY

CAUTION: DO NUT USE PUTTY OR PIPE DOPE, WARRANTY MAY BE VOIDED. TEFLON PIPE TAPE MAY BE USED BUT IS NOT NECESSARY ON THREADED CONNECTIONS.

1 Position pop-up flange (28) with foam gasket (27) in sink outlet. Attach mack washer (29) (flat side down), friction washer (30) and locknut (31). Do not tighten locknut at this time.

2 Attach tailpiece (32) to flange body, making sure o-ring is in tailpiece. Position assembly so the ball socket is toward back of sink then hand tighten locknut securely. Do not use putty.

3 Drop stopper (25) into drain opening. Insert ball rod (34) into ball socket and through hole in stopper tab. Slide ball nut (35) over ball rod and tighten. Do not overtighten.

4 Connect P-trap to tailpiece to pop-up assembly. Proceed to step (4) of faucet installation.
CAUTION: alignment of trap inlet and tailpiece is necessary to avoid damage.

Fig. 7-45. Installation instructions for attaching the tailpiece and pop-up to the sink (Courtesy of Nibco).

Fig. 7-46. A completed pop-up installation, showing the pivot rod and lift rod.

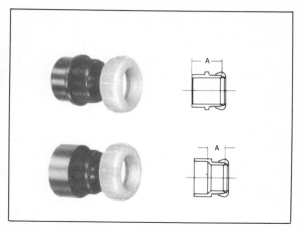

Fig. 7-47. Male (top) and female (bottom) fittings used to adapt a 1½-inch trap fitting to a 1¼-inch tailpiece (Courtesy of Nibco).

termine the alignment, then, if necessary, cut off the tailpiece and the drain line coming out of the wall to the correct length. Use a removable trap with a 1 ¼-inch inlet (Fig. 7-47), (to fit the tailpiece) and a 1 ½-inch outlet (that fits the drain line) and connect it to the two pipes.

For a double sink installation, the sinks are connected to each other first, then out into a single trap. Special tee kits are available at plumbing supply stores which have all the parts you need. If the drain line in the wall is centered between the sinks, use a center-outlet tee; if the drain is at one end, use an end-outlet tee.

Finally, install escutcheons and angle stops on the water lines. Use flexible water lines, which are available in different lengths, to connect the stops to the faucet.

Topping-Out Bathtubs and Showers

Since you have installed the bathtub or shower at the rough-in stage, all that's left to do now is top-out the faucets. Top-out will vary with the brand and style of the faucet, but is essentially a matter of installing the proper escutcheon or trim rings, the faucet handles, and the spout and showerhead. Complete instructions for the specific valve assembly you are using will be packed with the faucet.

Chapter 8

Electrical Wiring, Lighting, Ventilation, and Heat

A VERY IMPORTANT CONSIDERATION IN YOUR new bathroom is the safe installation of electrical wiring, including lights and outlets, and the addition of adequate heat and ventilation to ensure your comfort. Even in a room as small as a bathroom there is a fair amount of wiring that's necessary, and its installation must be planned just as carefully as any other phase of the construction.

During the planning and design process, your designer will probably suggest an outlet and lighting plan (Figs. 8-1 & 8-2), that will be convenient and adequate for your room layout. If you're doing your own design, you might have included already a possible wiring plan based on what's existing.

Now is a good time to go back and take another look at the "Likes and Dislikes" lists you made earlier, and make note of anything that is electrically related. Read through the suggestions in this chapter, and see how they relate to the bathroom you are building. When you are done, look over your designer's suggestions or your original wiring plan and make certain that the new layout meets your needs.

YOUR HOME'S ELECTRICAL SYSTEM

A basic understanding of how your home's electrical system is laid out and how it functions is very helpful if you intend to do any of the bathroom wiring yourself.

The electrical system begins with the service that is provided from your utility company. Most homes have a three-wire service, which either comes in from overhead or from underground. Two of the three wires are *hot*, in that they carry electricity all the time, and the third is a neutral wire, which is used to complete the electrical circuit. Each of the hot wires carries approximately 120 volts (the precise voltage varies with the utility company), while the neutral line carries no supply voltage. Combining the neutral wire with one of the hot wires provides a complete 120-volt circuit; combining the neutral with both of the hot wires provides a 240-volt circuit.

An Electrical Circuit

The complete path electricity takes is known as a *circuit*. In simple terms, the electricity flows out through the hot wire, into the appliance or other electrical device being used, then it flows back through the neutral wire. Each of the complete out and back revolutions is known as a *cycle*. In the United States, electrical service is *60 cycle*, mean-

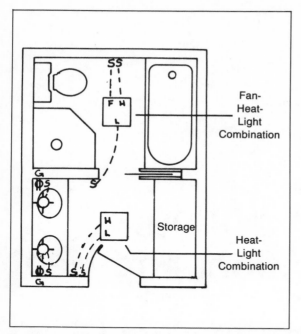

Fig. 8-1. An electrical layout for a typical family bathroom.

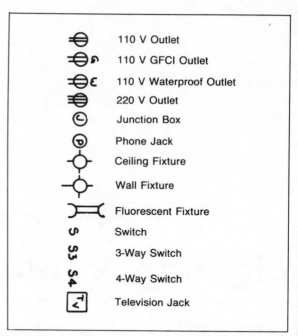

	110 V Outlet
	110 V GFCI Outlet
	110 V Waterproof Outlet
	220 V Outlet
	Junction Box
	Phone Jack
	Ceiling Fixture
	Wall Fixture
	Fluorescent Fixture
S	Switch
S3	3-Way Switch
S4	4-Way Switch
TV	Television Jack

Fig. 8-2. Standard electrical symbols used on plans.

ing it makes 60 complete out and back trips through the circuit each second.

Circuit Grounding

Every circuit has an additional wire known as the *ground wire*. Ground wires connect any metal portion of a fixture or appliance to the ground, usually through a water pipe or metal rod driven into the ground.

Ground wires offer protection against potentially dangerous electrical shock. Under normal circumstances, there isn't any electricity in the ground wire. If something goes wrong with a circuit, however, and the metal parts of the fixture become electrified, the excess electricity is carried safely off through the ground wire, preventing injury.

Ground Fault Circuit Interrupters

Ground fault circuit interrupters, (Fig. 8-3) commonly known as GFCIs, offer additional protection against accidental injury from electricity. A GFCI will react much faster to a fault in the circuit than the circuit breaker can, so it shuts down the circuit

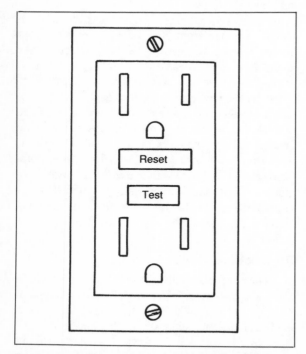

Fig. 8-3. A ground fault circuit interrupter (GFCI) outlet for use in the bathroom.

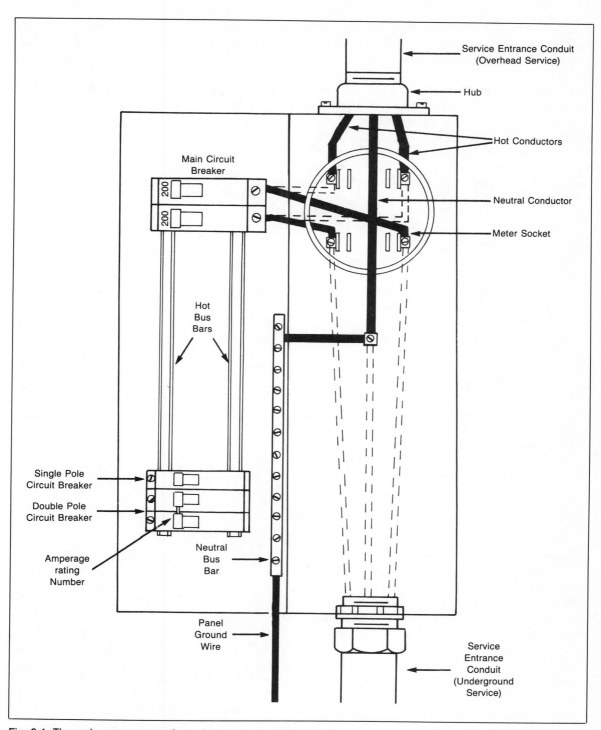

Fig. 8-4. The main components of a typical 200-amp service panel.

within about 1/40 second. The electrical code requires bathroom circuits be protected by a GFCI. This code is stringently enforced, and for your own protection it is one you do not want to ignore.

You can purchase GFCIs as an electrical outlet or as a circuit breaker. You install the circuit breaker in the service panel, and it protects all the devices on that circuit. When you install the GFCI outlet, which is more common, you can wire it in one of two ways: to protect the one outlet only, or to protect the one outlet and all the other outlets that are down-line from it. Each GFCI outlet includes complete wiring instructions.

The Service Panel

The service leads terminate in a box called the service panel. (See Fig. 8-4.) Within the panel is the *utility's meter*, which calculates and records how much electricity your home is using each month, the *main circuit breaker* which controls all the electricity coming into the panel, and the *circuit breakers* which control the individual circuits.

Also inside the panel, and hidden by the inside cover, are the hot and neutral bus bars and all the wiring connections. The *hot bus bars* are simply two flat metal bars, each is connected to a 120 volt hot wire from the main circuit breaker. The electrician will snap individual circuit breakers onto one or both of these bars, which allows them to tap off electricity to supply each circuit. A *single-pole circuit breaker* is one that contacts one bus bar only, providing a circuit of 120 volts. A *double-pole breaker* contacts both bars, and provides a 240-volt circuit.

The neutral bus bar contains a series of holes with screws threaded into the top of them. The electrician connects the main neutral service lead to the neutral bar, as he does the main panel ground wire, which is in turn secured to a cold-water pipe or grounding rod. He then secures neutral and ground wires from each individual circuit into one of the holes in the bar.

Color Coding

Color coding of electrical wires has become standardized over the years, and is required by the electrical codes. A wire with white insulation on the outside designates a neutral wire; a green (or bare wire) designates a ground; and any other color besides white or green, usually black or red, indicates a hot wire. Always use this system of color coding when installing new electrical wiring.

INSTALLING A NEW CIRCUIT

Although the inside of the service panel, with its confused mass of wires, might seem intimidating at first, installing a new circuit really is not difficult. Here are the basic steps:

☐ Determine the voltage and amperage of the circuit:

You will find this information printed on the side of motors and other such devices, or you can obtain it from your dealer.

☐ Route the new cable from the service panel to the bathroom:

Almost all the wiring done today is done with Type NM (nonmetallic) cable, which greatly simplifies the running of a new circuit. (See Figs. 8-5 & 8-6.) The cable contains one or more color-coded

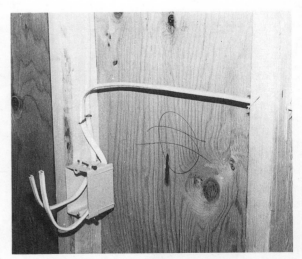

Fig. 8-5. Roughing-in a new outlet using Type NM cable and a plastic, nail-on electrical box. Note the amount of slack wire left at the box for making up the connections.

hot wires, a neutral wire, and a ground wire, all wrapped with a common outside insulating jacket.

You can purchase NM cable in different gauges (wire diameter) and with different numbers of hot wires, depending on its intended use. For a 120-volt circuit one hot wire is used, while most 240-volt circuits require two hot wires. To determine the gauge of the wire you need, refer to Table 8-1.

Enter the panel using conduit and conduit connectors, or with a cable connector through one of the knockouts, whichever is appropriate. Leave 2 to 3 feet of slack for making the connections.

☐ Connect the cable to the device it will serve:

Be certain you follow the color-coding, and also make sure you connect all ground wires. Certain mo-

tors, such as those for some spas (Fig. 8-7), require that you install a second ground wire on the motor housing. If you install a second ground wire, attach a ground clamp to any convenient cold water pipe and run a bare or green-jacketed wire between the clamp and the motor.

For safety, and to avoid confusion, all your ground wires must be topped out before the circuit is activated. Be sure you install all outlets, switches, fixtures, and other electrical devices on the circuit, and be sure all covers and safety plates are in place.

☐ Connect the cable to the circuit breaker:

First, shut off the main breaker, then remove the inside cover of the service panel to expose the wiring. With the main breaker off, the hot bus bars

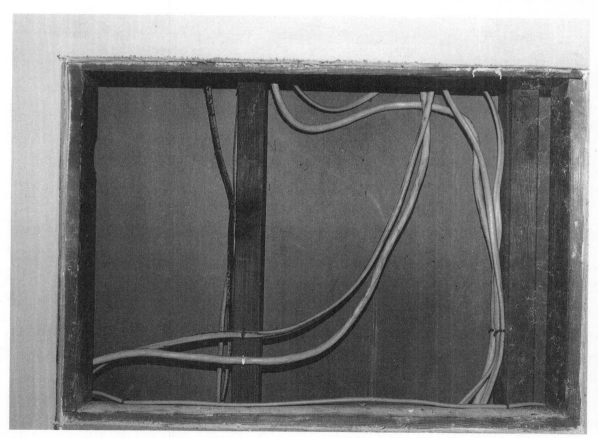

Fig. 8-6. Using the cut-out for a new medicine cabinet as a convenient opening for running new electrical cables.

Table 8-1. Determining Wire Gauge for Different Amp Circuits.

AMPERAGE OF CIRCUIT	WIRE GAUGE
15 amps	14
20 amps	12
30 amps	10
40 amps	8
50 amps	6

will not be carrying electricity. However, anything on the supply side of the breaker (the side coming from the meter) still will be live, so work carefully!

Double check to be sure the circuit breaker is the right one for the job—it should be a single pole for 120 volts or a double pole for 240 volts, and the amperage rating stamped on it should be the correct amperage for the circuit.

Snap the breaker into the bus bars in any open spot. Strip off the outer jacket of the cable, exposing the individual wires inside. Connect the hot wire(s) to the screw terminals on the circuit breaker, and connect the neutral and ground wires to any open terminals in the neutral bus bar. Remove the appropriate knockout on the panel cover, and replace the cover.

Check to be certain that you have topped out, everything on the circuit and that you have installed all the covers. Activate the circuit breaker, and check for proper operation of everything on the circuit. Finally, label what the circuit is used for on the inside panel cover, using an indelible marking pen.

ELECTRICAL OUTLETS

The bathroom contains few electrical outlets, and there is a reason for that. Outlets need to be con-

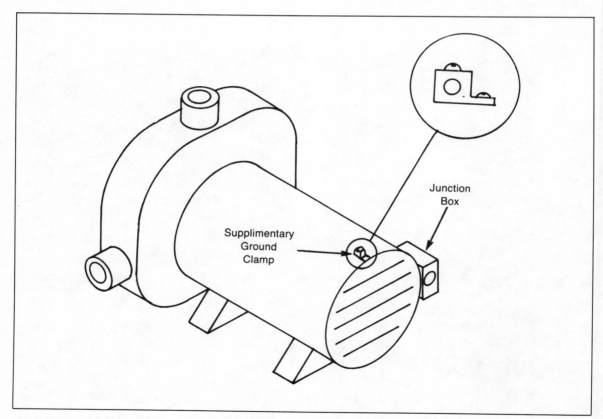

Fig. 8-7. The supplementary grounding attachment on a pump used with a whirlpool bathtub.

fined to the area adjacent to the sink, where you use electrical appliances such as razors and hair dryers. Outlets should not be anywhere around the bathtub or shower to avoid the risk of an electrical appliance coming into contact with the water in the tub.

Plan to provide one outlet at each sink in the room, even if the sinks are right next to each other. These outlets add convenience when two people are using the room at once, and prevents a cord from dangling over one sink in order to reach the other one. Remember that all outlets in the bathroom must be GFCI-protected.

BATHROOM LIGHTING

An adequate level of lighting in the bathroom (Fig. 8-8), is essential for safety and convenience, and adds to the style and beauty of the room. The following guidelines from the American Home Lighting Institute will help you determine your needs. Remember that these are the minimum acceptable light levels, and you might wish to exceed them in certain areas.

Sink and Mirror Under 36 Inches Wide

Place a ceiling fixture centered over the front edge of the sink, with a total of 100 to 120 watts of incandescent light or two 24-inch 40-watt fluorescent tubes. In addition to the ceiling fixture, provide a swag or wall light (Fig. 8-9), on either side of the mirror, 60 inches above the floor. If you are using incandescent lights, provide 75 watts in each fixture or use globe-shaped theatrical lighting strips with

Fig. 8-8. The proper lighting arrangement for a bathroom (Courtesy of the American Home Lighting Institute).

Fig. 8-9. Wall-mounted incandescent fixtures provide good lighting over the mirror and bathtub (Courtesy of Lightolier).

four to six bulbs per strip. For fluorescent lighting, provide one 24-inch 20-watt tube in each fixture.

Sink and Mirror Over 36 Inches Wide

Once again, you should place a ceiling fixture over the sink, with 120 watts of incandescent light or a double row of 36-inch 30-watt fluorescent tubes in a soffit box. An alternative is to use wall fixtures over the mirror, with three to four 60-watt bulbs in separate diffusers across the top of the mirror, or theatrical lighting with a minimum of six bulbs; for fluorescent lighting, provide two 36-inch 30-watt tubes or two 48-inch 40-watt tubes, placed behind diffusers over the mirror.

In the Bathtub or Shower

This often overlooked area needs good lighting for safety, especially if it is used by children, the elderly, or someone who is disabled. You should plan on a vapor-proof recessed ceiling fixture, centered over the tub or shower area, with a 60- to 75-watt incandescent bulb.

In the Toilet Compartment

This area is another often overlooked area that should have its own lighting source. Use a 60- to 75-watt incandescent ceiling or wall fixture, or a 30- to 40-watt fluorescent fixture.

Exterior Lighting

If you have an outside door that provides access between the bathroom and a spa or pool area, be sure you have a light fixture next to or over the door, plus floodlights to illuminate the spa area.

SWITCH LAYOUT

For convenience and energy efficiency, separate switches should be provided for different fixture groups in the bathroom. You should use one switch, near the door, for the main overhead lighting. If there are two doors into the room, use three-way switches and place one at each door.

Plan to provide separate switches at each sink, grouped with the outlets if desired, to control the fixtures over each of the mirrors. In addition, the fixture over the bathtub or shower, the fixture over the toilet, and any outside lights would each have its own switch.

A bath fan should have its own switch, as should an electric wall or ceiling heater. Combination fan/light/heat units usually come with a special triple switch that fits into a regular outlet box to simplify the wiring.

BUILDING A LIGHT BOX

A two- or three-sided box attached to the wall is simple to construct, and can be used to conceal fluorescent fixtures over the sink and mirror area. (See Fig. 8-10.) Make the box approximately 12 inches high, 18 to 24 inches deep, and long enough to be in proportion with the area you are illuminating.

You can build the sides out of plywood, painted or covered with wallpaper to match or contrast with the rest of the room, or you can use 1- x -12 lumber and stain it. The bottom frame should be built of 1- x -2 clear lumber, with plastic diffuser material, available at most hardware stores, used to conceal the fixtures and diffuse the light.

BATHROOM VENTILATION

Adequate ventilation is a must in the bathroom. High levels of moisture in the air can cause serious damage to wallcoverings, wooden windows and frames, wall framing, floorcoverings, and insulation, not to mention causing an annoying steaming-up of mirrors and windows.

If the bathroom has an operable window, additional ventilation is not required by most building codes. Windows do not always get opened however, especially in cold weather, and an exhaust fan is well worth considering. If the room has no operable windows, mechanical ventilation is required by code, and the codes might require that you tie the fan in with the light switch so that they both come on at the same time.

Ventilation in the bathroom is almost always accomplished through the use of a ceiling-mounted fan. (See Fig. 8-11.) You would attach the fan housing to the ceiling joists, at a level that places the bot-

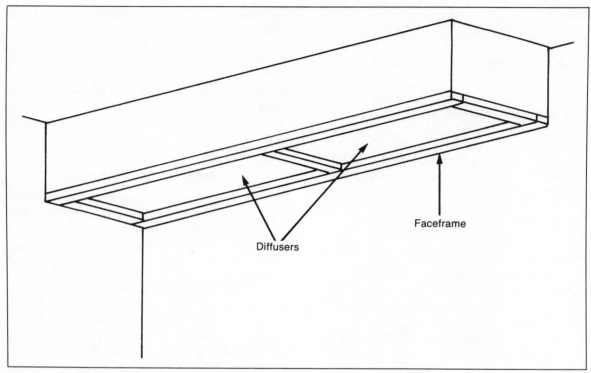

Fig. 8-10. A simple, custom-made light box for use over a vanity.

Faceframe

Diffusers

tom of the housing flush with the ceiling drywall. To conceal the fan and the edges of the drywall, attach a decorative louvered cover, usually chrome-plated metal or white plastic, to the housing. Bathroom fans are also available for direct, through the wall mounting if your bathroom is on an exterior wall. (See Fig. 8-12.)

Once you have installed the fan in the ceiling, you still must vent it to the outside (See Fig. 8-13). Installing the fan and then venting it into the attic simply moves the moisture problem from one area to another without eliminating it, and the moisture pushed in the attic by the fan can cause serious damage to wood and insulation.

Most fans have a 4-inch round opening with a spring-loaded damper, to which you connect the duct pipe. You can use flexible vinyl dryer hose for venting, provided it's accepted by your local building codes. Many codes require that you use flexible metal pipe instead. Attach the duct pipe to the fan

outlet with clamps or sheet metal screws, making certain the screws do not interfere with the damper, then seal the joint with duct tape. Cut an opening in the roof to accept the other end of the pipe, and install a capped roof flashing over the opening.

Your fan should have the capacity to change the air in the bathroom at least 8 times an hour, so you will need to perform some simple calculations: Multiply the bathroom's width by the length by the height to get the room's volume in cubic feet, then multiply by 8 to get the cubic feet of air per hour the fan will have to handle. Fans are rated in cubic feet per minute, so divide by 60 to convert from cubic feet per hour to cubic feet per minute (CFM).

When shopping for a fan, look for one with a CFM rating that meets your needs. If you have a long duct run, buy a fan with a little higher rating than what you need to compensate for the resistance of the pipe. Also, fans are rated for noise, so compare the sound ratings and look for a quiet one.

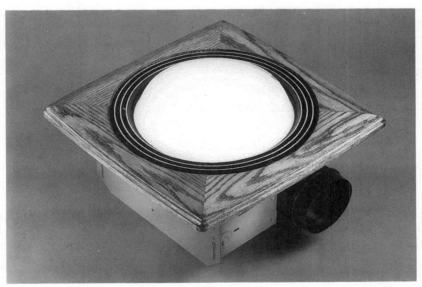

Fig. 8-11. Two examples of the many attractive fan-light combinations available for the bathroom. The round opening on the side of each of the units is the connection for the vent pipe, and also contains the damper assembly (Courtesy of Nutone Inc.).

Fig. 8-12. A through-the-wall vent fan for use on an exterior wall (Courtesy of Nutone, Inc.).

BATHROOM HEAT

Heat in the bathroom is something that is usually not considered until you're getting ready for work at 6 A.M. on a snowy January morning. Some definite comfort advantages to bathroom heat do exist, but the safety hazards make portable electric units a poor choice.

If you have a central forced air heating system, you might want to think about running a new duct into the bathroom. This duct can be brought up through the floor, through the ceiling, or, by installing a register in the toekick, even inside a cabinet.

If you do not have forced air heat, or if a new duct run is impractical, your best choice is a separate wall or ceiling heater. Wall heaters (Fig. 8-14), are available in both gas and electric models, with electric more commonly used because of the ease of installation. Select the location for a wall heater

Fig. 8-13. Using flexible dryer hose to vent a ceiling-mounted bath fan. A small dam will be constructed around the fan unit to keep it accessible when the new insulation is blown into the ceiling. (Note: not all building codes allow a fan to be vented using dryer hose.)

Fig. 8-14. An example of one of the many types of electric wall heaters suitable for use in the bathroom (Courtesy of NuTone Inc.).

Fig. 8-15. A fan-heat combination using infrared heat bulbs. If desired, a conventional floodlight bulb can be installed in place of one of the heat lamps to provide additional bathroom lighting (Courtesy of Nutone, Inc.).

Fig. 8-16. A ceiling-mounted fan-heat-light combination which uses electric coils and a small fan (in addition to the ventilation fan) for heating.

with care; avoid areas where someone might bump against it, or where a towel, curtain, or other flammable material might come into contact with it.

Some ceiling heaters have one or more infrared heat lamps in them (Fig. 8-15), radiant ceiling panels, as fan-forced, electric coils (Fig. 8-16), which is probably the most efficient and effective kind. You can purchase ceiling heaters in combination units that include a fan and/or a light fixture also, which lowers the cost and simplifies installation.

An option with most heaters is a timer, and it's worth considering. The timer will keep you from inadvertently leaving the heater on, which is a safety hazard and a waste of electricity.

Chapter 9

Basic Carpentry and Drywall

ALMOST EVERY REMODELING PROJECT, NO MATter how small, requires some carpentry and drywall skills. It might be only a few pieces of molding or a simple drywall patch, but you still need to know the proper tools and procedures to use. Each of the following sections will cover the basic skills needed for the aspects of remodeling that you are most likely to encounter.

REMOVING FRAMING

During remodeling, it might become necessary to remove part of the room's existing structure. While removing framing is not difficult, it needs to be approached with caution. Be sure you carefully study any framing you are about to tear out, and make absolutely certain that it does not support some other load. Check the attic in particular, and make certain any wall you intend to remove or alter does not have ceiling joists, roof supports, or other framing resting on it. In a two story house (Fig. 9-1), always assume that any first floor wall is load-bearing.

If you have determined that a wall is not load-bearing and you intend to remove it, first strip off the drywall. Cut through the tape in each corner and along the ceiling so you can remove the drywall without damaging the material on the adjacent walls.

With a reciprocating saw or handsaw, slice through each of the studs, then pull the cut halves off the nails in the top and bottom plates. If you want to reuse the studs, cut between the plate and the bottom of the stud using a reciprocating saw with a metal-cutting blade, then pull the entire stud down off the top nails. When all the studs are out, use a heavy wrecking bar to pry up the bottom plate, and to remove the two top plates.

To remove a load-bearing wall (Fig. 9-2), you need to first temporarily support the load that's on the wall—the ceiling joists for example—then transfer that load somewhere else after you have removed the wall. Begin by constructing a temporary wall on both sides of the wall you are removing. Place a 2-×-4 plate on the floor, and anchor it with two or three 16d nails. Place a second plate against the ceiling, hold it up by placing a few nails into the ceiling joists. Cut 2-×-4 studs that are about ¼ inch longer than the distance between the plates, then wedge them between the plates and toenail them in to prevent them from being dislodged. Remove the wall framing as outlined above.

You will need to install a beam to permanently support the ceiling joists. Beam sizing is dependent on the length of the area it has to span. You can get

145

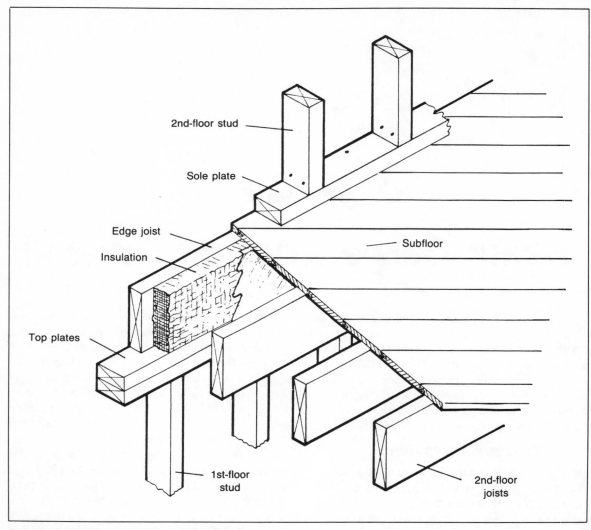

Fig. 9-1. Second floor joists in a two-story house.

the proper size for your opening by calling your local building department.

The easiest way to install the beam is to place it against the bottom of the ceiling joists, then install a 2- × -4 trimmer under each end to support it. (See ''framing openings'' following.) This type construction leaves the beam exposed below the ceiling, where it then can be drywalled or stained. If you want to conceal the beam in the attic, you will need to cut each ceiling joist in two places, creating a space between the cut ends that is wide enough

to accept the beam. Slip the beam up between the joists, rest it on trimmers or on the plates of the adjacent walls, then attach metal joist hangers to the beam to support the cut end of each joist. Slowly remove the temporary walls, watching to see that the beam accepts the new load without any problems.

FRAMING WALLS AND OPENINGS

A typical framed wall consists of a single 2- × -4 bottom plate, two top plates, and a series of vertical

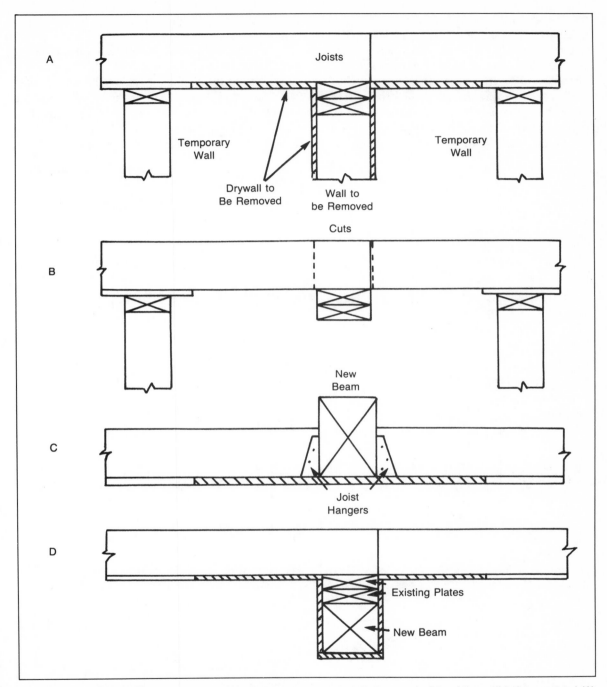

Fig. 9-2. Removing a load-bearing wall. Temporary supports are installed on each side of the wall being removed (A) and the drywall is stripped off the wall and a section of the ceiling. The joists then are cut on each side of the old wall plate (B), and a new beam is slipped in between the ends of the joists (C). An alternative method is to leave the joists uncut and the old top plates in place (D), then install a beam below the ceiling and cover it with drywall.

147

studs between them. (See Fig. 9-3.) During construction of a house, you frame the walls lying down, then tilt them up into position. In remodeling, usually there isn't any room to tilt up a finished wall, so the wall needs to be framed in place.

Begin by cutting the top and bottom plates to length. If this wall is to be a *partition wall* (one that does not carry any weight), you can eliminate the second top plate. Next, you will need to mark the

stud spacing—16 inches from center to center—on both plates.

First, measure over 15¼ inches from the left end of the plates (See Fig. 9-4.) (this location is where the edge of the first stud will be placed, making the stud's center 16 inches from the end of the plate). Use a square to mark a line across the face of both plates, then mark an X to the right of the line, indicating where the stud is to be placed. From

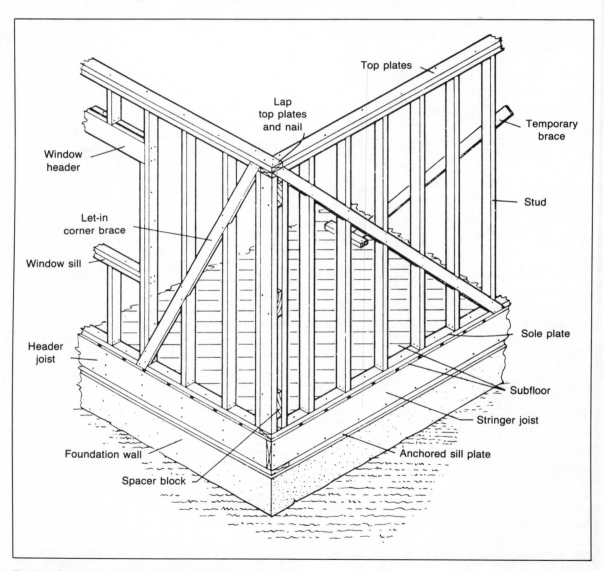

Fig. 9-3. Standard wall construction using platform framing.

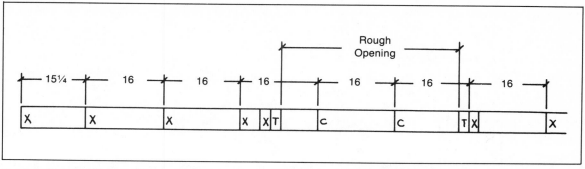

Fig. 9-4. Plate layout for studs on 16-inch centers. Note that regardless of the location of window openings, the spacing continues uninterrupted under it, with cripples (C) taking the place of the studs (X).

this first mark, measure and mark the full length of the plate in 16-inch increments, placing an X to the right side of each line to indicate where each stud is to be placed.

If the wall is to have an opening for a door, window, medicine cabinet, or other object, you will need to know the required rough opening size, which you can obtain from your dealer. The rough opening dimensions are the size that you frame the opening, so there is enough clearance for whatever's going into the opening.

A framed opening (Fig. 9-5) requires a header, which carries the load over the opening, and two king studs and trimmers that form the sides of the opening and also support the header. If the opening does not go all the way to the floor, you also will need a sill at the bottom of the opening.

To lay out the opening on the plates, first mark where the center of the opening will be. Next, measure half of the opening's width to each side of center, which is where the inside edges of the trimmers will be. The original 16-inch spacing marks that you laid out before now indicate where the cripples will be, so that the 16-inch spacing is maintained for the entire wall, regardless of where the opening falls.

To assemble the wall, first nail the bottom plate to the floor. Cut the studs to length and place one at each end of the plate. Carefully plumb the studs using a spirit level and attach them to the adjacent cross walls. You might need to open a section of each cross wall and install blocking between the studs to have something to which you nail the new wall. Finally, place the top plate on the end studs, nail it

into the ceiling joists, then toenail in the remaining studs.

FRAMING AN OPENING INTO AN EXISTING WALL

A situation that often arises in remodeling is the need to frame an opening into an existing wall, for a new window or doorway, or perhaps for a recessed medicine cabinet. (See Fig. 9-6.)

The first framing step is to get access to the existing framing. Mark the size of the opening on the wall, then locate and mark the first stud past the opening on each side. Next, mark a horizontal line between the studs, about 6 inches down from the ceiling (this procedure leaves you a piece of existing drywall to tape to, without having to disturb the ceiling). Use a reciprocating saw or hand drywall saw to cut through the drywall along this line, and down the edge of the two studs, all the way to the floor.

Determine where the top of the opening is to be placed, measure up from there the height of the header, and cut the studs at that point. Repeat the procedure at the bottom of the opening, allowing for the thickness of the sill. Nail a trimmer to each of the existing studs. Install the header so that it rests on the trimmers, and toenail the cut studs to it. Toenail in two new trimmers, carefully plumbed, where the sides of the opening will be located. Next, install a sill across the tops of the cut studs on the bottom of the opening. Finally, cut along the insides of the framing and remove the drywall from the back of the opening (unless it's for a medicine cabinet, in which case the back drywall remains), which

149

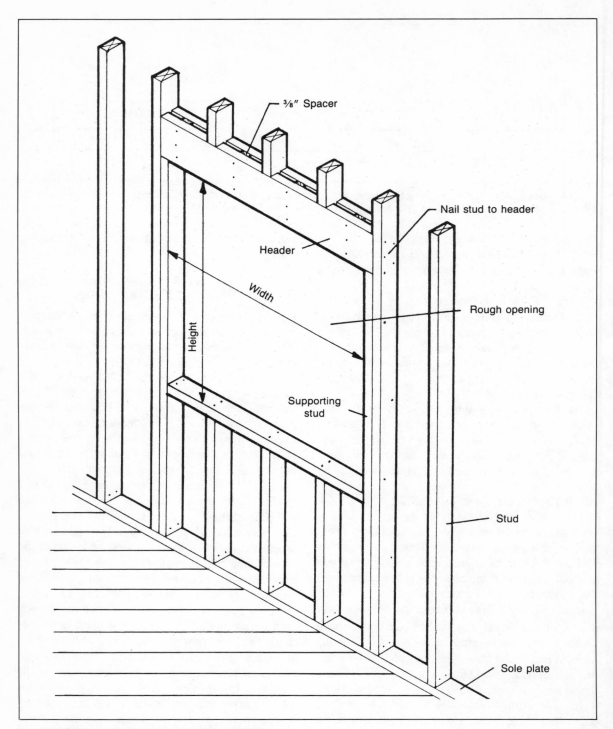

Fig. 9-5. Standard framing for a window opening.

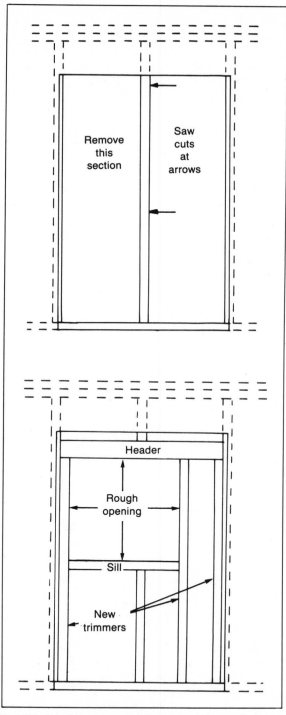

Fig. 9-6. Framing an opening into an existing wall.

leaves you with drywall patches on one side of the wall only.

INSTALLING DOORS

If your plans call for a new hinged door in an existing door frame, you should remove the hinge pins and take out the door, leaving the frame and hinges in place. Take the door to any door supplier. They can cut and mortise a new door to the exact dimensions of the old one, including boring the holes for the lockset. Then simply transfer the hinge halves from the old door to the new one, put the door into the existing frame, and reinstall the hinge pins.

Prehung Doors

If you need a new door and frame, either for a new opening or an existing one, you will find that a prehung unit greatly simplifies the installation. When you order the door, you will need to know several things:

☐ How wide do you want the door? The most common sizes are sold in 2-inch increments from 2 to 3 feet.
☐ How high do you want the door? (6 foot 8 inches is standard).
☐ How thick do you want your door? Standard thicknesses are usually 1⅜ inches for interior doors, 1¾ inches for exterior doors.
☐ How wide are the jambs? The standard jamb width is 4⁹⁄₁₆ inches, which allows for a 2 × 4 stud wall with ½ inch drywall on each side.
☐ Which way will the door swing?

Installing a prehung door is quite simple. Place the unit in the opening, and use a level to plumb the jamb with the hinges. Tapered wooden shims, driven in from both sides between the jamb and the framing, allow you to make adjustments. (See Fig. 9-7.) When this jamb is plumb, nail through the jamb and the shims into the framing, using 8d or 10d finish nails. Level and plumb the other jamb leg, using shims as necessary to get a uniform line between the closed door and the jambs. Secure the other ver-

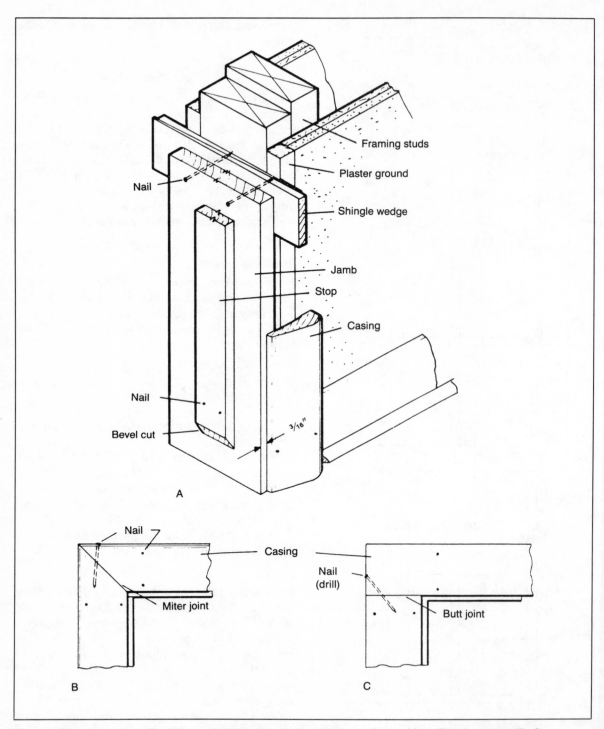

Fig. 9-7. The components of a prehung door installation (A), and two methods of installing the casing (B, C).

tical jamb leg with finish nails, then finish off the installation with pieces of casing, which hide the gap between the jambs and the framing.

Pocket Doors

Occasionally, you will find there simply is not enough room for a regular hinged door to open, so a pocket door must be used. Pocket doors utilize a frame, or pocket, which is enclosed in the wall. You mount the door on rollers and hang it from a top track. (See Fig. 9-8.) When opened, the door disappears into the wall, taking up no floor space. Pocket door frames are made to fit a 2-×-4 wall, and are available readily in pocket depths that fit a 2-0, 2-4, 2-6, 2-8, or 3-0 door.

Obtain the proper rough opening size from your dealer, and frame the opening in the wall, using a header full length over the entire opening. The pocket frame usually is shipped in three pieces; the pocket frame, the top track, and one jamb leg. Set

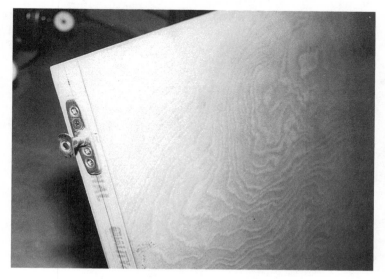

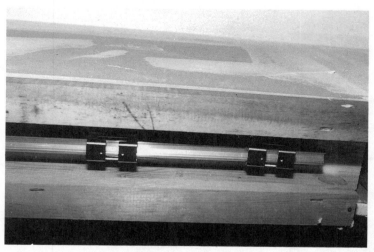

Fig. 9-8. Attaching the hanger hardware to the top of a door that will be used in a pocket frame (top). The pocket frame (bottom) contains a track and rollers from which the door is hung.

the top track in place (it will slip right into notches in the frame) and secure it with nails. Attach the jamb leg to the end of the top track, and slide the assembled unit into the opening.

Using shims, carefully plumb the back of the frame and the jamb leg. Secure the frame by nailing down through the front bracket into the floor, and through the jamb and the back of the frame into the trimmers. Follow the manufacturer's instructions and mount the roller hardware on top of the door. Holding the door at an angle, with bottom toward you, hook the rollers onto the track. Using a small wrench, adjust the rollers until the door is high enough above the floor to slide easily, and the edge of the door meets the jamb leg along its entire length. Install a pocket door latch on the front edge of the door.

You should install the drywall carefully over the pocket frame. Construction adhesive is the best answer, since the sides of the frame are difficult to nail into. If you use nails, be certain they're short enough so they do not go all the way through the frame and into the door.

After you have drywalled the wall, finish off the installation with the four trim pieces that were supplied with the door. Mount the two short pieces to

Fig. 9-9. A high-quality operable skylight, which is ideal for both light and ventilation (Courtesy of Andersen Corporation).

the top track board, flush with the drywall on each side. Mount the two long pieces on the front of the frame, where they prevent the door from swinging out into the room. Be certain the trim pieces do not rub against the door, binding or restricting its movement. Use casing to finish off the opening on each side.

SKYLIGHTS

Skylights (Fig. 9-9), are ideal for getting additional natural light into a bathroom, giving it a bright, open feeling. If you have an attic above your ceiling, you will need to construct a shaft between the skylight and the ceiling to bring in the light. (See Fig. 9-10.)

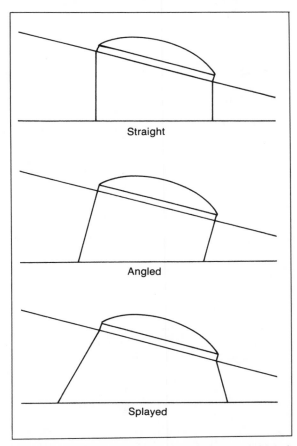

Fig. 9-10. Common types of skylight shafts. The straight shaft (top) is the easiest to build but lets in the least light. The splayed shaft (bottom) can be built with any desired ceiling opening size to maximize the amount of light being admitted.

If you have an open ceiling, in which the ceiling is actually the underside of the roof, a hole is all that's required. (See Fig. 9-11.) Try to choose a skylight size that will fit between the rafters to simplify the installation. If your home has roof trusses, the trusses cannot be cut, so the skylight must fit between them.

Mark out the desired opening on the ceiling. If you are using a shaft, the ceiling opening can be larger than the size of the skylight to admit more light. Cut and remove the drywall, then frame the ceiling opening. If you need to cut ceiling joists, first support the ceiling with temporary walls as outlined above. Frame between the next two uncut joists (Fig. 9-12), and attach the ends of the cut joists to the new framing.

Using the ceiling opening as a guide, frame the roof opening to the manufacturer's specifications. Remove the shingles in this area, and cut out the sheathing. Skylights vary in the way you install them, so again following the manufacturer's instructions, construct a raised box (called a *curb*) on the roof. Patch in the shingles, using the recommended flashing on all four sides of the curb, then mount the skylight to the curb.

Connect each of the four corners of the roof opening to the four corners of the ceiling opening, using 2 × 4s either flat or on edge. If either opening is larger than 2 feet on a side, install intermediate 2 × 4s. Finish off the shaft with drywall on the inside, painted white to reflect the most light. Remember to insulate the attic side of the shaft to at least R-11 to minimize heat loss.

DRYWALL REPAIRS

Drywall repairs (Fig. 9-13), are a necessary part of almost every job, but do not let them scare you off. With a little practice, the techniques are easy to learn. In addition to your regular tools, you also will need a 6-inch taping knife, a 12-inch taping knife, and a taping pan.

Begin by squaring up any holes in the existing drywall, and cut them back to the centers of the nearest studs. A little time spent here will simplify greatly the patching. Next, cut patches from new drywall to fit the openings. Drywall is cut by placing

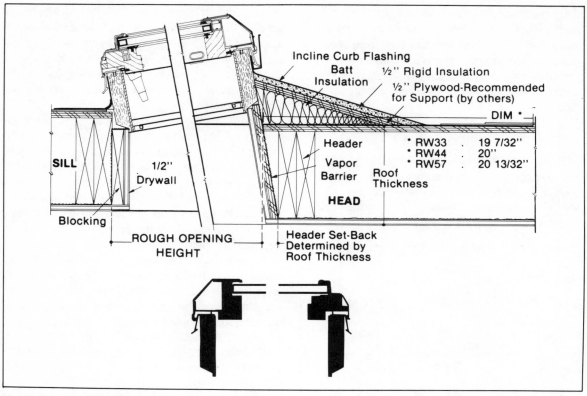

Fig. 9-11. A skylight and skylight shaft for use where there is no attic space above the ceiling (Courtesy of Andersen Corporation).

Labels in Fig. 9-11:

Incline Curb Flashing
Batt Insulation
½'' Rigid Insulation
½'' Plywood-Recommended for Support (by others)
DIM *

SILL
½'' Drywall
Blocking
ROUGH OPENING HEIGHT

Header
Vapor Barrier
Roof Thickness
HEAD

* RW33	.	19 7/32''
* RW44	.	20''
* RW57	.	20 13/32''

Header Set-Back Determined by Roof Thickness

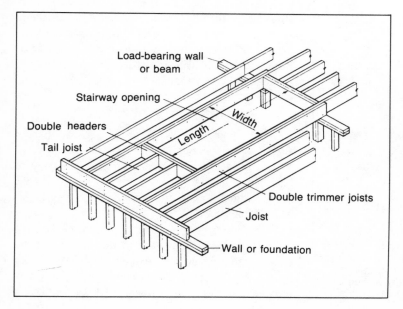

Fig. 9-12. Construction details for framing an opening in a ceiling, prior to constructing the skylight shaft.

Labels in Fig. 9-12:

Load-bearing wall or beam
Stairway opening
Double headers
Tail joist
Width
Length
Double trimmer joists
Joist
Wall or foundation

a straightedge along the intended line of the cut, on the face side of the sheet, and then cutting through the face paper with a utility knife. Sharply snap the cut piece downward to break the gypsum core, then cut through the back paper to separate the piece.

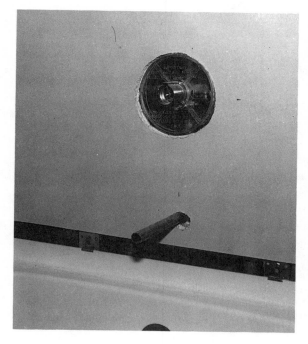

Fig. 9-13. Two of the many drywall patches commonly encountered in bathroom remodeling, including a new sheet of drywall over the new mixer valve (top) and a recess for a toilet paper holder (bottom).

Secure the patches in place with drywall screws or cup-head drywall nails to secure them.

Taping is the first step. (See Fig. 9-14.) Use a premixed joint compound that is labeled "taping" or "general purpose" and paper drywall tape. Place the compound in the pan, and use your 6-inch blade to place a layer of compound over the seam of the patch. Place a piece of tape in the compound, centered over the line of the seam. Starting from one end, hold your blade at about a 45 degree angle and draw it along the tape, imbedding the tape in the compound. Smooth the tape out and press it firmly against the drywall, removing the excess joint compound as you go. When you have taped all the seams, let them dry overnight.

Using general purpose or "topping" compound, go over each of the tape seams the next day. Use your 12-inch blade, held at a flatter angle than you used when taping. The topping should completely cover the taped seam, feathering out to a thin line on the wall to either side of the seam. Let the topping dry, then sand it smooth. If necessary, apply a second topping coat, feathering it out past the edges of the previous coat.

Covering Corners

For inside corners, apply taping compound to the wall on each side of the corner. Fold the tape along the center crease and press it into the corner, using your taping knife as described above. Using a 6-inch blade or a special corner trowel, apply the topping compound to each side of the corner.

Use a metal corner bead to cover the outside corners. Place the bead over the corner, center it, then nail through the punched flanges on each side. Working from the top down, hold your 6-inch blade on both the bead and the wall and apply taping compound to cover the metal. Let it dry overnight, then use your 12-inch blade in the same manner to top over the taping compound.

Texturing Drywall

If you are going to paint the drywall, you can texture it to help hide the seams and add an interesting decorative touch. You can apply texturing in a

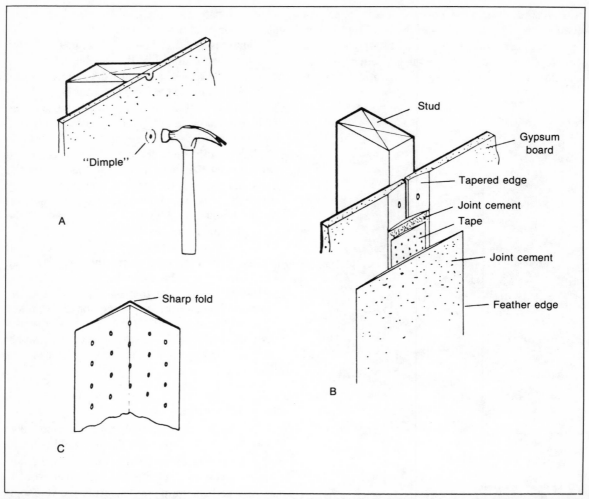

Fig. 9-14. Drywall details. Use your hammer to "dimple" the nailhead just below the surface of the drywall (A) to allow it to be concealed with joint compound. (B) shows the steps involved in taping and topping a joint, and (C) illustrates how the joint tape is folded for use in an inside corner.

number of different ways, so experiment in an out-of-the-way corner and see what you like:

☐ Thin the joint compound with water, add a very small amount of fine sand, then apply it with a 12-inch blade held lightly against the wall. This blade will apply the compound in irregular patches, called *skip troweling*;

☐ Dip a broom or stiff brush in thinned compound,

then run a stick across the bristles, "flicking" thin globs of compound on the wall;

☐ Apply joint compound to the walls with a sponge, stiff brush, crumpled paper, or other objects to create interesting patterns;

☐ Add texturing sand, available at most paint stores, to paint and roll it onto the wall when you apply the paint, creating a light, bumpy sand texture.

Chapter 10

Cabinets and Accessories

M ANY MANUFACTURERS WERE QUICK TO SPOT the rapidly growing trend toward more colorful and luxurious bathrooms, and it was not long before they designed new items solely for bathroom comfort, convenience, and enjoyment and placed them on the market. The result has been an exciting array of products that run the gamut from soaps and bubble baths to oak cabinets and high-tech electronics. All over the country, new shops are springing up that cater to accessories for the bathroom, and rarely do you find a major department store that does not have a large and intriguing bath department.

In this chapter, you will become acquainted with some of the many cabinets, fittings, and accessories that are available for finishing off the interior of your bathroom. The next step is up to you and your imagination!

CABINETS

Your choices for the interior of the bathroom begin with the type cabinetry you will be using, and there are lots of options. The basic bathroom cabinet is the vanity, which provides badly-needed bathroom storage space while offering a support for the countertop and sink. Many plumbing supply houses sell

vanity packages, which include the vanity cabinet and a one-piece sink/counter with backsplash.

If you plan on installing more than just a vanity cabinet, check the catalogs from the kitchen cabinet manufacturers. (See Fig. 10-1.) These companies have learned that their cabinets are just as much at home in the bathroom as they are in the kitchen, and most offer a full line of cabinets designed exclusively for the bath. In addition to vanities, you will find desk units that are open underneath (Fig. 10-2), designed to serve as a sit-down makeup area; floor to ceiling storage cabinets (Fig. 10-3); open shelving kits; and all sorts of moldings and other parts to help you create a beautifully finished bathroom.

Installing a Vanity Cabinet

Cabinet installation is very simple and straightforward, requiring basic tools and a little patience. To install a basic vanity cabinet, first remove the baseboards in the area where the cabinet will sit. If the floor is to be underlayed (see Chapter 11) in preparation for new floorcovering, the cabinet should be installed after the underlayment but before the flooring. (See Fig. 10-4.)

Measure the width of the cabinet and mark its

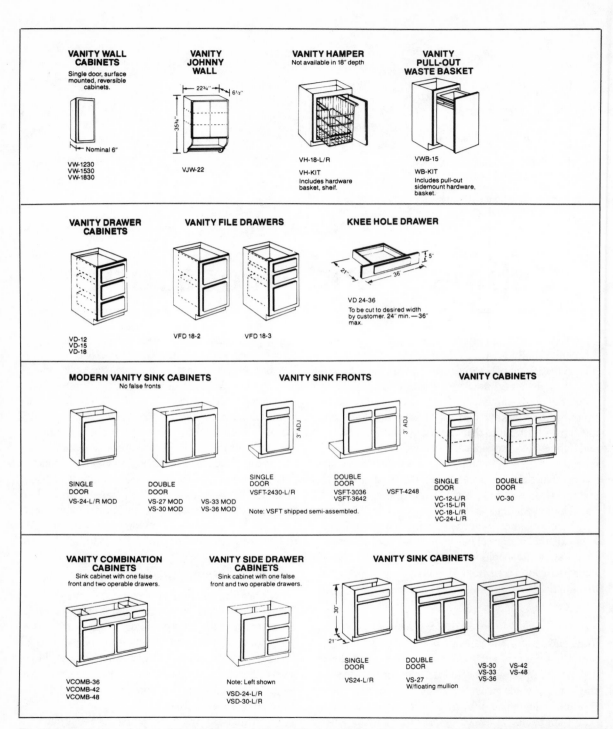

VANITY WALL CABINETS

Single door, surface mounted, reversible cabinets.

Nominal 6"

VW-1230
VW-1530
VW-1830

VANITY JOHNNY WALL

22¾" 6½"

35¼"

VJW-22

VANITY HAMPER

Not available in 18" depth

VH-18-L/R

VH-KIT
Includes hardware basket, shelf.

VANITY PULL-OUT WASTE BASKET

VWB-15

WB-KIT
Includes pull-out sidemount hardware, basket.

VANITY DRAWER CABINETS

VD-12
VD-15
VD-18

VANITY FILE DRAWERS

VFD 18-2   VFD 18-3

KNEE HOLE DRAWER

21   36   5"

VD 24-36

To be cut to desired width by customer. 24" min. — 36" max.

MODERN VANITY SINK CABINETS

No false fronts

SINGLE DOOR
VS-24-L/R MOD

DOUBLE DOOR
VS-27 MOD   VS-33 MOD
VS-30 MOD   VS-36 MOD

VANITY SINK FRONTS

3" ADJ

SINGLE DOOR
VSFT-2430-L/R

3" ADJ

DOUBLE DOOR
VSFT-3036
VSFT-3642   VSFT-4248

Note: VSFT shipped semi-assembled.

VANITY CABINETS

SINGLE DOOR
VC-12-L/R
VC-15-L/R
VC-18-L/R
VC-24-L/R

DOUBLE DOOR
VC-30

VANITY COMBINATION CABINETS

Sink cabinet with one false front and two operable drawers.

VCOMB-36
VCOMB-42
VCOMB-48

VANITY SIDE DRAWER CABINETS

Sink cabinet with one false front and two operable drawers.

Note: Left shown
VSD-24-L/R
VSD-30-L/R

VANITY SINK CABINETS

30"

21"

SINGLE DOOR
VS24-L/R

DOUBLE DOOR
VS-27
W/floating mullion

VS-30   VS-42
VS-33   VS-48
VS-36

Fig. 10-1. A selection of some of the vanities and other cabinets available for use in the bathroom (Courtesy of Diamond Cabinets).

160

Fig. 10-2. An example of how different modular cabinets can be combined into an attractive wall unit that maximizes storage space (Courtesy of Medallion Kitchens).

Fig. 10-3. A floor-to-ceiling bank of built-in storage cabinets which match the vanity cabinet (Courtesy of Kitchen Kompact).

centerline on the cabinet's back. Mark the wall where the center of the cabinet will be placed. Measure from the wall centerline mark to each of the pipes, and transfer these measurements to the back of the cabinet. Measure up from the floor to each of the pipes, and transfer these measurements also. Drill a small hole through the back of the cabinets at the center of each pipe location. Finally, measure the diameter of each of the pipes, and using the small holes as guides, drill full-size holes in the cabinet back. Drill through from the inside of the cabinet to prevent splintering the back.

Slip the cabinet over the pipes and slide it against the wall. Use a level to check the cabinet side to side and front to back, and also along one side to see if it's plumb. You can use tapered wooden shims as necessary to bring the cabinet plumb and level. When you have the cabinet where you want it, drill through the back at the top, into the studs. Secure the cabinet to the wall with wood screws.

MEDICINE CABINETS

The standard bathroom storage area is the medicine cabinet. For most people it doesn't have enough storage space, necessitating the installation of a vanity cabinet, but the medicine cabinet still has a definite place in today's bathroom. Medicine cabinets offer convenient storage for small health and grooming aids, and most also provide a mirror.

You can purchase medicine cabinets in colors and styles that will suit any bathroom decor. They are available with sliding mirrored doors, bi-, tri-, and quad-fold mirrored doors (Fig. 10-5), swinging mirrored doors (Fig. 10-6), or with no mirror at all. Several types have built-in lights also (Fig. 10-7), eliminating the need for an additional fixture.

Most medicine cabinets can be surface mounted or mounted in a recess in the wall. Surface mounting is much easier, but recessed mounting gives the cabinet a cleaner, finished appearance. To surface mount a medicine cabinet, you need to first locate the studs. The cabinet will have predrilled holes or slots in the back, and if they line up with the studs after you've positioned the cabinet, fine. If not, you will need to drill new holes through the back in the proper places. Secure the cabinet to the wall with at least four screws driven into the studs, two at the top and two at the bottom.

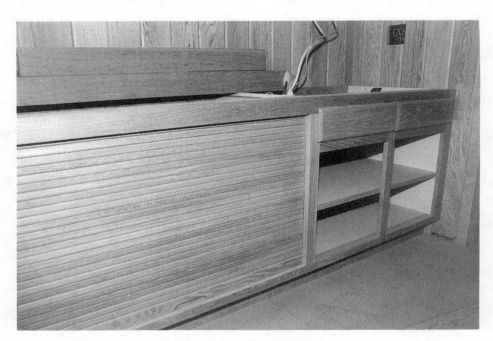

Fig. 10-4. A custom bathroom cabinet, installed prior to the finish flooring.

Fig. 10-5. A sleek, unframed medicine cabinet with three mirrored doors (Courtesy of NuTone, Inc.).

Fig. 10-6. A recessed medicine cabinet with a wood-framed, mirrored door (Courtesy of NuTone, Inc.).

For a recessed cabinet, you will need to make an opening in the wall. Many medicine cabinets are made to fit between the studs, which simplifies the installation—all you have to do is cut an appropriate sized hole in the drywall. If your cabinet would end up off-center when you placed it between the studs, or if the cabinet is larger than one stud space, you will need to frame an opening as described in Chapter 9. When you have the opening in the wall, slip the medicine cabinet into place and secure it with two screws on each side, driven into the studs.

COUNTERS

You have several options in countertop material also, and your final choice depends on your decorating scheme, the type sink you have selected, and your own personal preferences. The following sections discuss the four materials used most often.

Ceramic Tile

Tile gives an elegant look to any room, and it

Fig. 10-7. This cabinet, with wood trim and three mirrored doors, also features a good amount of built-in lighting (Courtesy of NuTone, Inc.).

is especially at home in the bathroom. Literally thousands of combinations of color, size, and style exist, so finding one that suits your bathroom should not be too difficult. Tile is also durable and stain resistant, and, except for the grout lines, easy to keep clean.

Ceramic tile usually is set over a mortar base, which requires professional installation. (See Fig. 10-8.) It also can be set by a do-it-yourselfer, using tile adhesive on a plywood base. Plaster spacers and easy-to-use tile cutters greatly simplify the installation. Most tile suppliers can supply all your needs, including complete instruction sheets and use of a tile cutter at little or no charge.

With ceramic tile, most people use a surface-mounted, self-rimming sink. You can set the sink level with the top of the cabinet, then tile it into place.

Plastic Laminates

Another material that has come a long way in recent years is plastic laminate. (See Fig. 10-9.) Laminate counters are durable and very easy to clean, and resist most stains. You will find a huge selection of colors and patterns, and several different edge and backsplash configurations are available. (See Fig. 10-10.)

Another plus for laminate counters is the ease of installation. Have the counter made to your specifications, then simply set it on the vanity and screw up from underneath to secure it. You then set the backsplash in place against the wall with adhesive, and cut out the sink hole with a jig saw. Self-rimming sinks work best with this type of counter, set in place with adhesive caulking. A sink and sink rim also can be used, but the rim is difficult to keep clean and also detracts from the beauty of the counter.

If you are using a patterned laminate, try to look at a large sample, not just a chip. Some of the patterns can overpower a small room when installed, which really is not apparent when you look at a small sample.

Synthetic Marble

Synthetic marble is another popular and attrac-

COUNTERTOPS
Wood Base
Glass Mesh Mortar Unit C513-87

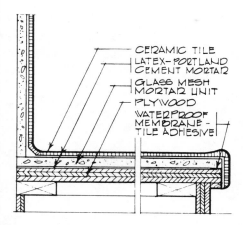

CERAMIC TILE
LATEX-PORTLAND CEMENT MORTAR
GLASS MESH MORTAR UNIT
PLYWOOD
WATERPROOF MEMBRANE - TILE ADHESIVE

All specifications for ceramic tile installations must conform to local building codes, ordinances, trade practices and climatic conditions.

Cement Mortar   C511-87   **Thin-Bed**   C512-87

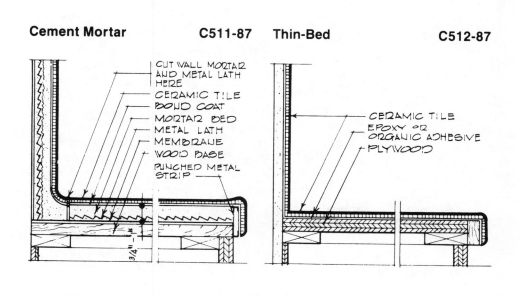

CUT WALL MORTAR AND METAL LATH HERE
CERAMIC TILE
BOND COAT
MORTAR BED
METAL LATH
MEMBRANE
WOOD BASE
PUNCHED METAL STRIP

3/4"

CERAMIC TILE
EPOXY OR ORGANIC ADHESIVE
PLYWOOD

Fig. 10-8. Details of mortar- and adhesive-bed ceramic tile countertop installations (Courtesy of the Tile Council of America).

tive material for counters, and fits especially well with a somewhat more formal bathroom. It is durable and easy to clean, and its seamless construction eliminates dirt-gathering cracks.

Synthetic marble counters usually are made with an integral sink, but they also can be purchased with a sink hole that can be used with a self-rimming sink.

Corian

This DuPont product is one of the most durable for bathroom use. (See Fig. 10-11 and 10-12.)

It is water and stain resistant, and stubborn surface marks can be removed with fine grit sandpaper. You can purchase Corian with an integral sink or with a sink hole, again for a self-rimming sink. The drawbacks to Corian are its relatively high cost, about twice that of ceramic tile, and its limited color selection. Once again, try to look at a large sample.

TUB AND SHOWER DOORS

Virtually all stall showers and tub/shower combinations require an enclosure to keep the water con-

Fig. 10-9. An innovative use of plastic laminates to cover two corner cabinets in this small guest bathroom (Courtesy of Wilsonart).

tained. One attractive solution is the use of a tub or shower door. When you begin shopping for a new tub or shower door, you will quickly discover the new emphasis on beautifully decorated bathrooms has not been overlooked here, either. Sleek chrome-, brass- and gold-plated metal frames are all readily available, and dozens of designs and colors are available for the glass portion of the door also.

Manufacturers construct shower doors today with top and bottom pivots on one side, and the doors swing out for access to the tub. Tub doors, on the other hand, are most commonly available as a two-door unit that slides horizontally in a track. Vertically-sliding tub doors also are available, a real advantage when bathing children since the entire width of the bathtub is accessible.

Fig. 10-10. Some of the common edge treatments for plastic laminate countertops (Courtesy of Wilsonart).

When you are shopping for a door, you will want to look for some common characteristics. Because of the danger of slipping in the tub or shower and falling against the door, all tub and shower doors must be constructed of safety glass. Some less expensive doors are made of plastic, but in the long run, you'll be happier and more satisfied with a good quality glass unit.

Frosted glass is the most common door material, which affords the tub or shower user more privacy. Clear glass units also are available, which have the advantage of not obscuring the beauty of your tub or shower enclosure. The disadvantage to clear glass is that it requires constant maintenance to keep it free of water spots.

Tub doors, and especially shower doors, might

Fig. 10-11. Installing a Corian countertop and backsplashes. The two thin strips of wood keep pressure on the backsplash end pieces until the adhesive sets.

Fig. 10-12. A look at one of the types of Corian edge treatments available. This one uses a natural wood strip inset into a groove in the counter's front edge.

prove a little tricky for the inexperienced do-it-yourselfer, so you might want to consider having the glass company do the installation. They know how to size and adjust the door to correctly fit the opening, and they'll see that the frame is properly caulked and securely attached to the walls.

SHOWER CURTAINS

Shower curtains, an old favorite in many bathrooms, offer a colorful option for containing the water in a combination tub/shower unit. Hundreds of curtains are available from which to choose, and many are available with matching draperies to cover the windows and tie backs are available to hold the shower curtain alongside the tub. Many manufacturers are offering wider shower curtains to fit today's popular oversize tubs.

You mount the shower curtain on a metal rod, which is held in place by a bracket on each end. Different types of brackets are available, including

Fig. 10-13. Sliding mirrored closet doors provide a tremendous amount of full-length mirror area in the bathroom or dressing room (Courtesy of Monarch Mirror Doors).

169

ones that attach to the wall with screws and others that expand to press against the walls and hold the curtain rod up by friction. The standard rod is chrome-plated, but you also can find brass- and gold-plated models. Many bathroom accessory shops sell plastic slip-on rod covers in a variety of colors, along with colored hooks for mounting the curtain on the rod.

MIRROR DOORS

If your new bathroom or master bedroom suite in-cludes a closet, you might want to consider a set of mirror doors for it. These doors offer the advan-tage of a wide, floor to ceiling mirror for a full-length view when dressing.

Mirror doors are available as double doors which slide past each other horizontally in top and bottom tracks (Fig. 10-13), or as two- and four-panel bifold units (Fig. 10-14). Once again, chrome-, brass-, and gold-plated frames are available.

The mirror door units come in several stan-dard sizes and are designed to fit specific closet

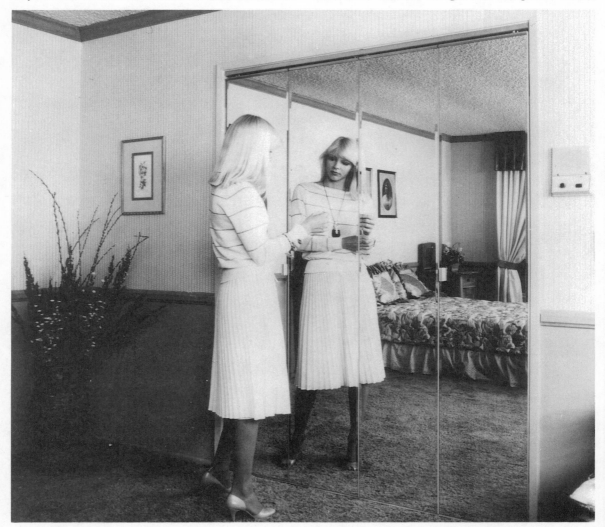

Fig. 10-14. Bifold mirror doors offer easy access into the closet while still providing a great amount of full-length mirror area (Courtesy of Monarch Mirror Doors).

Fig. 10-15. A space-saving, multi-level towel rack (Courtesy of Nutone Inc.).

openings, whether the opening is wrapped with drywall or finished with wood jambs and casing. It's best to consult with your dealer for the proper finished opening size before framing the closet.

ACCESSORIES

Purchasing accessories for your bathroom is one of the really fun parts of remodeling, and with the huge selection of products from which to choose, there is something to match every decor and budget. An accessory does not need to be big or expensive to find a place in your bathroom. In fact, many of the most colorful, ingenious, practical, and eye-catching accessories in any successful bathroom were purchased for under $20.00 each! Just use your imagination, watch the sales, and add pieces one at a time.

Check out a bathroom shop or department store catalog the next time you have the chance, and treat yourself to an afternoon of truly enjoyable shopping for your new bathroom. You will find elegant towel racks, colorful glasses and soap dishes, wall murals, magazine racks, padded toilet seats, wall-mounted hair dryers, storage cabinets and shelves that fit just about anywhere, soaps and bath oils in every conceivable scent, plush towels in every size from wash-

Fig. 10-16. A selection of some of the common sizes and styles of chrome-plated grab bars for use in the shower, bathtub, and other bathroom areas (Courtesy of NuTone, Inc.).

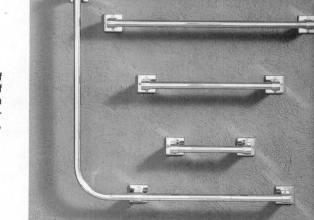

cloth to bath sheet, and much, much more. (See Figs. 10-15 through 10-20.)

PLANTS

A beautiful, low-cost way to dress up a bathroom is through the use of live plants. Many types of plants thrive in the bathroom's environment of warmth and high humidity, and no matter what your decor, the lush green foliage adds an unbeatable decorating touch.

Depending on the orientation of your bathroom's exterior wall and the amount of floor space with which you have to work, you might want to consider an actual garden in the bathroom. (See

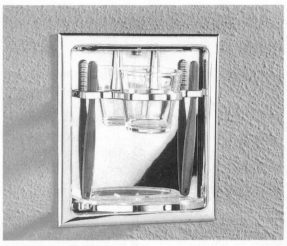

Fig. 10-17. A recessed glass, soap, and toothbrush holder, which revolve out of sight when not in use (Courtesy of Nu-Tone, Inc.).

Fig. 10-18. A stylish and convenient magazine rack for use next to the toilet (Courtesy of NuTone, Inc.).

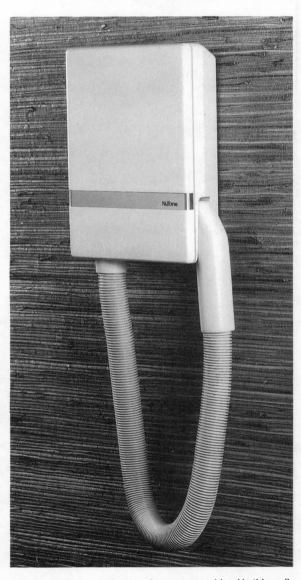

Fig. 10-19. Safety and convenience are combined in this wall-mounted hair dryer, which has no hand-held electric parts (Courtesy of NuTone, Inc.).

172

Fig. 10-20. A handy bathroom clothes line, which retracts into the holder at left when not in use (Courtesy of NuTone, Inc.).

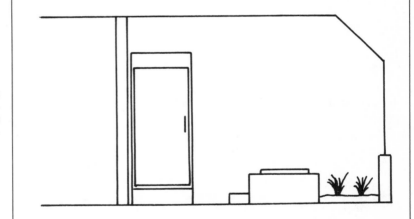

Fig. 10-21. A small garden behind a raised bathtub platform is right at home in the bathroom. The prefabricated greenhouse window admits abundant natural light for a bright, open room and good plant growth.

Fig. 10-21.) Placing plants between the bathtub and the window creates a natural privacy break, gives the plants plenty of light and moisture, and makes a relaxing backdrop for the bather. A hose bib in the garden area simplifies watering, or you might even wish to install a drip irrigation system on a timer.

Another effective design strategy is to place a garden outside the bathroom, directly in front of a large window. (See Fig. 10-22.) A privacy fence shields the garden and the window from view, and creates a secluded, intimate oasis for the bather.

If a full-fledged garden is not in your plans, simple potted plant arrangements for the bathroom are well worth considering. For large bathrooms, try placing several plants in individual containers, then arranging them in a gardenlike grouping. Rearranging the plants or substituting new ones, especially flowering plants in seasonal bloom, allows for instant redecorating and a continually new look in the room.

Smaller bathrooms can benefit from plants also. Small potted plants can be placed on the vanity or the back of the toilet, or on short open shelves. And

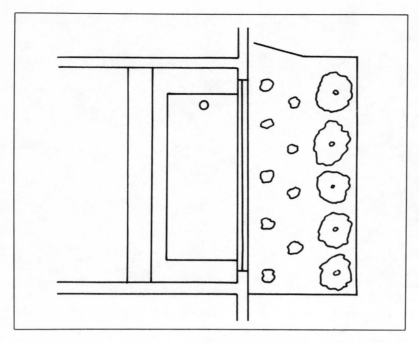

Fig. 10-22. An outside garden, located next to a large bathroom window, easily brings the outdoors inside. The three-sided fence and gate ensure privacy, and by placing larger plants at the back of the garden, the fence eventually will be concealed with greenery.

Table 10-1. House Plants for Bathroom Use.

COMMON NAME	LATIN NAME	COMMON NAME	LATIN NAME
African linden	*Sparmannia africana*	hydrangeas	*Hydrangea macrophylla*
arrowhead plant	*Syngonium podophyllum*	lipstick plant	*Aeschynanthus radicans*
asparagus fern	*Asparagus setaceus*	maidenhair fern	*Adiantum tenerum*
avocado	genus *Persea*	mosaic plant	genus *Fittonia*
baby's tears	*Helxine urticaceae*	moss fern	genus *Selaginella*
bead plant	*Nertera granadensis*	Norfolk pine	*Araucaria neterophylla*
black-eyed Susan	genus *Thunbergia*	passionflower	genus *Passiflora*
bridal flower	genus *Stephanotis*	piggyback plant	*Tolmiea menziesii*
busy Lizzie	*Impatiens sultanii*	pigmy date palm	*Phoenix roebelenii*
cast-iron plant	*Aspidistra elatior*	prayer plant	*Maranta leuconeura*
Chinese evergreen	*Aglaonema modestum*	rice cactus	*Rhipsalis paradoxa*
Christmas cactus	*Zygocactus truncatus*	roundleaf fern	*Pellaea rotundifolia*
coffee plant	*Coffea arabica*	spider plant	*Chlorophytum comosum*
coleus	*Coleus hybridus*	split-leaf philodendron	*Monstera deliciosa*
coral berry	*Ardisia crenata*	Sprenger asparagus	*Asparagus densiflorus*
creeping fig	*Ficus pumila*	Sprengeri	*Asparagus sprengeri*
dumb cane	*Dieffenbachia maculata*	staghorn fern	genus *Platycerium*
elephant's ear	*Colocasia esculenta*	Swedish ivy	*Plentranthus oert*
Easter cactus	*Rhipsalidopsis gaertneri*	sweet alyssum	*Lobularia maritima*
English ivy	*Hedera helix*	sweetheart ivy	*Hedera helix*
grape ivy	*Cissus rhombifolia*	sweet potato	*Ipomoea batatas*
hare's foot fern	*Polypodium aureum*	trailing velvet plant	*Ruellia makoyana*
holly fern	genus *Polystichum*	velvet passion	genus *Gynura*
		wandering Jew	*Tradescantia fluminensis* or *Zebrina pendula*

Hanging plants are always at home in a bathroom.

Your bathroom does not need to be bathed in natural light; many plants thrive in windowless rooms also. Plant lights or a combination of warm and soft fluorescent lights are often all that is needed to keep your plants healthy. If necessary, the plants can be rotated out of the bathroom to a sunny window for a short time, then brought back in.

Table 10-1 lists a number of plants that should do very well in the bathroom; consult with your nurseryman for help in selecting the best ones for your particular situation.

Chapter 11

Coloring the Bathroom

WITH THE BATHROOM PLUMBED, WIRED, AND ENclosed, the real fun can begin! Drab, one-color bathrooms are a thing of the past, as you will learn in this chapter; decorating your new bathroom is exciting and challenging, and you should lavish as much care on it as you would any other room of the house. Bright and bold or subtle and peaceful, the choices are yours. Your imagination and your budget are the only limits!

CREATING A UNIQUE LOOK

As you have seen emphasized throughout this book, today's bathroom is no longer the stark, drab, utilitarian room it once was. An abundance of colors and patterns are seen everywhere in the bathroom, and each room makes an individual statement that reflects you and your lifestyle.

Don't be timid about experimenting with different colors in the bathroom; usually the worst that can happen is that you have to paint or paper over them. One of the nice things about a bathroom is its modest size; you usually only need a small amount of material, so even the most lavish wall and floor coverings are within reach of your pocketbook.

Early on, even as early as the initial design stage, you might want to visualize and create a specific "look" for the bathroom. The look might be one that compliments and continues a specific decorating scheme in the rest of the house, or you might choose to have the bathroom be its own unique, individual space. You might want a guest bathroom that is elegantly formal, or a master bathroom that is straight out of an equatorial rain forest. Whatever you visualize, deciding on it early can be a big help in selecting and coordinating tile, cabinets, fixtures, and other materials, and even in choosing the overall layout and configuration of the room.

The following sections discuss a few of the many bathroom design motifs that are possible, with the key factors that distinguish each of them.

Country

The simple charm of the country look (Fig. 11-1), is becoming increasingly popular, offering a rural haven in the heart of the city. Large windows open up the room and bring in lots of light. Woodwork, preferably in oak, fir or pine, should be kept fairly light. Antiques and other collectibles look good, giving the room a homey and perhaps slightly cluttered look. Pale blues, yellows, and greens are good as accent colors, but keep it simple and casual.

Fig. 11-1. A rustic, open feeling is achieved with the exposed beams and high ceilings in the country bathroom (Courtesy of American Standard).

European

The frameless cabinets first popularized in Europe give this design its name. Cabinet doors are usually off-white laminate with wood trim. (See Fig. 11-2.) The room's overall appearance is rather sleek and uncluttered. The primary colors are cream and parchment, with strategic accents of bold colors to keep the bathroom from becoming too stark.

Formal

Formal bathrooms have a slightly cold and reserved feeling, with medium to dark wood tones and understated accent colors. Much of the room's elegance comes from the carefully chosen accessories, including brass or gold faucets and towel bars. Synthetic marble works well for counters and tub enclosures, as does Corian.

Mediterranean

The Mediterranean bathroom is on the heavy and somewhat dark side. White, thickly textured walls look good, with dark, rough wood and olive green or red accents. Wall-mounted light fixtures that resemble candles and sconces are a nice touch, as are unpolished towel bars and accessories with a rough hewn look, typically in pewter or cast iron. When decorating a bathroom in the Mediterranean style, care must be taken not to let the room become too dark, oppressive, or closed in.

Fig. 11-2. European frameless cabinetry offers a clean, sleek look to this contemporary bathroom design (Courtesy of Kitchen Kompact).

Modern

The modern bathroom usually is characterized by bright, glossy accent colors against a white background. Polished chrome faucets and accessories look good, and you might even opt for boldly colored fixtures or an alternating black and white look.

Oriental

To achieve an Oriental look in your bathroom, stick with the traditional colors of polished black with red accents. Shiny, polished brass faucets and towel bars will work fine, as will painted moldings and trim with an Oriental feel. Black lacquered accessories fit right in, and you can select from a wide variety of colorful Oriental artwork for the walls.

Rain Forest

The look best described as "rain forest" creates a lush, relaxing atmosphere in the bathroom. The color scheme is predominantly green, with floral print wallpaper and pale green fixtures. Plants abound, particularly ferns and dwarf, broadleaf trees, and a slow-moving wood and cane paddle fan on the ceiling adds a nice touch. Once again, with this type of decor, be careful that you do not overdo it and close the room in.

Turn-of-the-Century

Turn-of-the-century is another popular bathroom look which, like the country bathroom, is reminiscent of a slower way of life. Polished wood wainscotting works nicely, with off-white paint or a lightly patterned wallpaper with an off-white background on the wall above the wood. Antique oak cabinets and dull brass faucets look nice. You might also consider an antique (or reproduction) claw-foot bathtub and pull-chain toilet to really complete the feeling of days gone by.

DECORATING HELP FOR PROBLEM ROOMS

Good decorating can do more than just brighten up a room. With a little care and thought, certain decorating strategies can be used to trick the eye into overlooking a room's shortcomings.

Narrow Room

Horizontal stripes on the wallcovering will widen a narrow room, as will the strategic use of mirrors on the narrow wall to give a feeling of depth.

Small Room

Keep the small bathroom open and light. Avoid closely patterned, dark wallpaper and dark paint. Once again large mirrors will help, as will white and cool pastel colors. Be consistent with your color scheme, and minimize contrasts.

Warm or Cool Room

Cool, subtle greens and blues will tend to cool down a warm room, as will deep green plants. For the cool room, perk it up with warm tones of red and yellow.

WALL COVERINGS

One of the fun things about a bathroom is that just about any wall or floor covering will work well in it. For example, natural wood siding, stained or painted to any color that suits your decor, is right at home in the bathroom. Or you might want to try a 3- or 4-foot-high wood wainscotting with paint or wallpaper above it. Wood and tile work well together, as does tile with paint or wallpaper.

Hand-painted designs or stenciling against a white wall makes a beautiful border at the ceiling, as does a 4- or 6-inch border of wallpaper. Lots of combinations of materials and colors work well together, so experiment a little!

Paint

Paint is still the most popular decorating material in the bathroom, and thousands of stock and custom-mixed colors exist from which to choose. Use semigloss paint, which has additives in it that make it more water resistant and easier to clean than flat paint.

Latex paint is fine for the walls and ceiling, but be sure you prime new drywall before applying the finish coat. For previously painted walls, wash them well with TSP and water, and lightly sand glossy

Fig. 11-3. High-quality, cushioned no-wax linoleum is always right at home in any style of bathroom (Courtesy of Congoleum Corporation).

areas to give the new paint better adhesion. For woodwork, use an oil-based paint for best results and smoothest finish. Aklyd resin, an alcohol and acid blend, is the most common of the oil based paints in use today, and will give you a nice finish with no brush marks.

Make it a rule to purchase the best quality paint and painting tools you can afford. They'll pay you back with easier use, better hiding power, long life, and a beautiful finish.

Wallpaper

Wallpaper is becoming another excellent choice for bathroom decorating. An incredible range of choices in colors and patterns exists, from a simple, sedate print in muted colors to bold stripes of color or lush green tropical foliage. With a little patience, even a beginner can wallpaper a room with beautiful results. When you purchase your wallpaper, your dealer can provide you with a simple checklist of tools and other supplies you will need, which can be purchased inexpensively.

Most wallpapers will work fine in the bathroom, with the exception of flocked papers and some grass-clothes, which do not hold up well in the bathroom's humidity. If you have any questions about the suitability of a particular wallpaper for use in the bathroom, ask your dealer.

Do-it-yourselfers usually find that prepasted paper is the easiest for them to use. The paper simply is cut to length, dipped in a water tray to activate the paste, then applied to the wall. Dry papers, which are coated with premixed adhesive, are available also. They are usually a little lower in cost, and their application is not that much more difficult than applying prepasted paper.

FLOOR COVERINGS

Several different floorcovering materials can be used which will work well in the bathroom. (See Figs. 11-3 through 11-5.) Do-it-yourself installation is possible with just about all of them, or your floorcovering dealer can arrange for professional installation. Here again, the bathroom's small size works in its favor,

Fig. 11-4. In this bathroom, wall-to-wall carpeting was extended up over the step and onto the bathtub platform, creating a warm and elegant room.

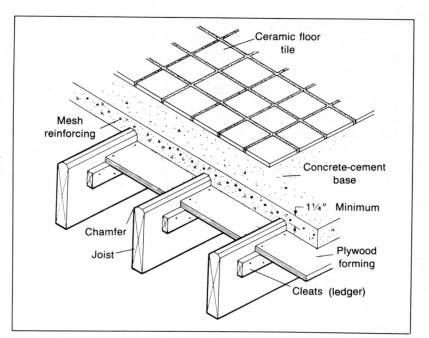

Fig. 11-5. Construction details for the installation of a mortar-base ceramic tile floor.

Ceramic floor tile

Mesh reinforcing

Concrete-cement base

1¼" Minimum

Chamfer

Joist

Plywood forming

Cleats (ledger)

Table 11-1. Bathroom Floor-covering Materials.

MATERIAL	ADVANTAGES	DISADVANTAGES	INSTALLATION DIFFICULTY
LINOLEUM	easy to clean; many colors and patterns; cushioned and no-wax available wide rolls—usually no seams in bathroom;	cold; moderately hard under foot	easy to moderate; difficult if coved
CERAMIC TILE	durable; rich appearance; many colors and patterns	cold; hard; slippery; grout lines difficult to clean	moderate to difficult
CARPET	warm underfoot; rich appearance; soft; nonslip; no visible seams	can hold water; can hold odors; some types might mildew; shows traffic wear	easy to moderate
FLOOR	easiest installation; cushioned and no-wax available	cold; moderately hard; many seams	easy
TILE HARD WOOD	durable; rich, warm color	cold; hard; slippery; difficult to maintain	moderate to difficult

minimizing both material and installation costs. For a comparison of the advantages and disadvantages of different types of floor coverings, see Table 11-1.

FLOOR UNDERLAYMENT

If you are installing new flooring over a rough subfloor, or over old linoleum or floor tile, you should underlay the floor first. The usual choice for under-

layment among professionals is ⅜-inch particleboard. It is inexpensive, readily available, easy to cut and nail, and provides a smooth surface with good adhesion for the new floor.

Particleboard is sold in 4- × -8-foot sheets. You can lay it in either direction, but plan your installation to minimize seams. Space each sheet about 1/16 inch apart, and use 6d ring shank nails or coated, air-driven staples to install it.

Appendix

For more information on some of the products and services available to help you remodel your bathroom, write to the following:

Amerec, A Division of Nasscor
(Saunas and steam equipment)
P.O. Box 40569
Bellevue, WA 98004

American Home Lighting Institute
(Lighting information)
435 N. Michigan Ave.
Chicago, IL 60611-4067

American Olean Tile Company
(Ceramic tile)
1000 Cannon Ave.
P.O. Box 271
Lansdale, PA 19446-0271

American Plywood Association
(Plywood)
P.O. Box 11700
Tacoma, WA 98411

American Standard
(Bathroom and kitchen fixtures)
3 Crossroads of Commerce
Suite 100
Rolling Meadows, IL 60008

Andersen Corporation
(Windows and skylights)
Bayport, MN 55003

Channellock, Inc.
(Tools)
1306 South Main St.
P.O. Box 519
Meadville, PA 16335-0519

Congoleum Corporation
(Floor coverings)
Resilient Flooring Division
195 Belgrove Dr.
Kearny, NJ 07032

Cultured Marble Institute
(Cultured Marble information)
435 N. Michigan Ave.
Chicago, IL 60611-4067

Diamond Cabinets
(Bathroom cabinets)
P.O. Box 547
Hillsboro, OR 97123

E.I. DuPont de Nemours Company, Inc.
(Corian)
Corian Building Products
Wilmington, DE 19898

Fluidmaster, Inc.
(Bathroom fittings and repair parts)
P.O. Box 4264
1800 Via Burton
Anaheim, CA 92803

Lattner Boiler Company
(Steam generators and equipment)
1411 Ninth St. SW
P.O. Box 1527
Cedar Rapids, IA 52406

Lightolier
(Lighting products)
100 Lighting Way
Secaucus, NJ 07094

Medallion Kitchens of Minnesota
(Bathroom cabinets)
180 Industrial Blvd.
Waconia, MN 55387

Microphor, Inc.
(Water-saving fixtures and faucets)
452 East Hill Rd.
P.O. Box 1460
Willits, CA 95490

Moen, A Division of Stanadyne
(Faucets)
377 Woodland Ave.
Elyria, OH 44036-2111

Monarch Mirror Door Company
(Mirror doors)
21325 Superior St.
P.O. Box 4118
Chatsworth, CA 91313-4118

Glastec
A Division of Riblet Products Corporation
(Bathroom fixtures)
11832 CR 14
P.O. Box 28
Middlebury, IN 46540

Helo Sauna and Fitness, Inc.
(Saunas and steam equipment)
28 Fahey St.
Stamford, CT 06907

Interbath Inc.
(Bathroom faucets and fixtures)
427 N. Baldwin Park Blvd.
City of Industry, CA 91746-1491

Jacuzzi Whirlpool Bath
(Whirlpool baths and spas)
P.O. Drawer J
Walnut Creek, CA 94596

Kitchen Kompact, Inc.
(Bathroom cabinets)
KK Plaza
P.O. Box 868
Jeffersonville, IN 47131

Kohler Company
(Bathroom and kitchen fixtures)
Kohler, WI 53044

Nibco, Inc.
(Plumbing supplies)
P.O. Box 1167
Elkhart, IN 46515

Nutone Products
(Bathroom accessories)
Madison & Red Bank Rds.
Cincinnati, OH 45227

Philips Industries Inc.
(Bathroom fixtures)
Lasco Division
3255 E Miraloma Ave.
Anaheim, CA 92806

Plumbing Manufacturer's Institute
(General information)
Building C, Suite 20
800 Roosevelt Rd.
Glen Ellyn, IL 60137

Sancor Industries, Ltd.
(Composting toilets)
140-30 Milner Ave.
Scarborough, Ontario, Canada M1S 3R3

Tile Council of America, Inc.
(Ceramic tile information)
P.O. Box 326
Princeton, NJ 08542-0326

Tylo Sauna and Steam
(Saunas and steam equipment)
5 Westchester Plaza
Elmsford, NY 10523

Universal-Rundle Corporation
(Bathroom and kitchen fixtures)
303 North St.
P.O. Box 29
New Castle, PA 16103

Wallcovering Information Bureau
(General information)
66 Morris Ave.
Springfield, NJ 07081

Western Wood Products Association
(Wood types and uses)
522 SW Fifth Ave.
Portland, OR 97204-2122

Wilsonart Laminates
(Plastic laminates)
600 General Bruce Dr.
Temple, TX 76501

Wood Moulding and Millwork Producers
(Moulding information)
P.O. Box 25278
Portland, OR 97225

Index

Index

Edited by Nina Barr

Other Bestsellers From TAB

☐ **TROUBLESHOOTING AND REPAIRING VCRs—Gordon McComb**

It's estimated that 50% of all American households today have at least one VCR. *Newsweek* magazine reports that most service operations charge a minimum of $40 just to look at a machine, and in some areas there's a minimum repair charge of $95 *plus the cost of any parts*. Now this time- and money-saving sourcebook gives you complete schematics and step-by-step details on general up-keep and repair of home VCRs—from the simple cleaning and lubricating of parts, to troubleshooting power and circuitry problems. 336 pp., 300 illus.

Paper $18.95   **Hard $24.95**
Book No. 2960

☐ **THE ILLUSTRATED HOME ELECTRONICS FIX-IT BOOK—2nd Edition—Homer L. Davidson**

This revised edition of the bestselling home electronics fix-it handbook will save you time and aggravation AND money! It is the only repair manual you will ever need to fix most household electronic equipment. Packed with how-to illustrations that any novice can follow, you'll soon be able to fix that broken television and portable stereo/cassette player and "Boom Box" and intercom and . . . the list goes on! 480 pp., 377 illus.

Paper $19.95   **Hard $25.95**
Book No. 2883

☐ **SUNSPACES—HOME ADDITIONS FOR YEAR-ROUND NATURAL LIVING—John Mauldin, Photography by John H. Mauldin and Juan L. Espinosa**

Have you been thinking of enclosing your porch to increase your living space? Want to add a family room, but want the best use of the space for the money? Do you want information on solar energy and ideas on how you can make it work in your home? If "yes" is your answer to any of these questions, you'll want to own this fascinating guide! 256 pp., 179 illus.

Paper $17.95   **Hard $21.95**
Book No. 2816

☐ **MAJOR HOME APPLIANCES: A Common Sense Repair Manual—Darell L. Rains**

Prolong the life and efficiency of your major appliances . . . save hundreds of dollars in appliance servicing and repair costs . . . eliminate the frustration of having to wait days, even weeks, until you can get a serviceman in to repair it! With the help and advice of service professional Darell L. Rains, even the most inexperienced home handyman can easily keep any washer, dryer, refrigerator, icemaker, or dishwasher working at top efficiency year after year! 160 pp., 387 illus.

Paper $16.95   **Hard $21.95**
Book No. 2747

☐ **TROUBLESHOOTING AND REPAIRING SMALL HOME APPLIANCES—Bob Wood**

Author Bob Wood pairs step-by-step pictures with detailed instructions on how to fix 43 of the most common electric appliances found in the home. Following the illustrations and directions provided, you'll be able to quickly disassemble practically any electrical device to get to the trouble source. Among those included are: drill, garbage disposal, can opener, grass trimmer, vacuum cleaner, blender, and much more! Telltale symptoms, troubleshooting techniques, maintenance measures—even operating tests and instruments—are included for each fix-it project featured. 256 pp., 473 Illus.

Paper $18.95   **Hard $23.95**
Book No. 2912

☐ **DREAM HOMES: 66 PLANS TO MAKE YOUR DREAMS COME TRUE—Jerold L. Axelrod**

If you are planning on—or just dreaming of—building a new home, you will find this book completely fascinating. Compiled by a well-known architect whose home designs have been featured regularly in the syndicated "House of the Week" and *Home* magazine, this beautifully bound volume presents one of the finest collections of luxury home designs ever assembled in a single volume! 86 pp., 201 illus., 8 1/2″ × 11″, 20 pp. of full-color illus.

Paper $23.95   **Hard $29.95**
Book No. 2829

☐ **ADD A ROOM: A PRACTICAL GUIDE TO EXPANDING YOUR HOME—Paul Bianchina**

Overflowing with helpful diagrams, photographs, and illustrations, this indispensable guide focuses on the professional details that make the difference between a room addition that blends in and one that looks like an afterthought. It's far more than a volume of plans or architectural ideas . . . it's a complete how-to-do-it manual that leaves no question unanswered. The types of rooms you can build using this guide include a garage, a room on top of your garage, a sunspace or greenhouse, a family or rec room, a bathroom, and many others. 400 pp., 360 illus.

Paper $19.95   **Hard $27.95**
Book No. 2811

☐ **62 HOME REMOTE CONTROL AND AUTOMATION PROJECTS—Delton T. Horn**

Here are 62 different remote control and automation units that anyone can build. All parts and components are readily obtainable and the cost is only a fraction of that charged for ready-built devices in electronics stores . . . some of the devices can't be purchased commercially at any price! Just think how you can make your home safer and more convenient with these devices. 294 pp., 222 illus., Paperback.

Paper $11.95   **Hard $13.95**
Book No. 2735

Other Bestsellers From TAB